Sunset

Making Your Home
Child-Safe

Safety at home means attention to details, such
as a low guard rail to prevent baby from rolling off
the changing table. But don't rely on the railing:
stay with baby every minute.

By Don Vandervort
with the Editors of Sunset Books
and Sunset Magazine

Lane Publishing Co. ■ Menlo Park, California

When They're into Everything

Accidents happen, occasionally, to everyone. But when little ones creep, climb, toddle, and scamper through the house, the accident rate usually goes up. Children themselves, innocent, inquisitive, and into everything, are half the equation. The other half shows up in our homes in ordinary circumstances—a lamp that tips, a tablecloth that drapes, laundry detergent left within sight and reach.

Taking you on an in-depth childproofing tour, room by room and area by area, this book shows how you can make your home and outdoor property safer for young children.

Safety gate (see page 63) keeps him off stairs when not accompanied by a grownup.

Note, however, that the safety information in this book is not intended as a substitute for your personal supervision of the child. Never leave a child unattended, even in the most carefully childproofed environment. No book can cover every conceivable present or future hazard to children. The publisher will not be legally liable for injuries, losses, or property damage due to omissions or errors in this book.

For reviewing the text and graphics and advising on safety, we give special thanks to Hans Grigo of the National Safety Council.

Thanks also to the following for their valuable help with research and checking: American Red Cross, Pasadena Chapter; Tom Conrad of the California State Automobile Association; Jamie E. Haines of the National Fire Protection Agency; H. James Holroyd, M.D., American Academy of Pediatrics; Alan Tani, M.D., of the San Francisco Poison Control Center; and Elaine Tyrrel of the U.S. Consumer Product Safety Commission. For their generous assistance with props for our photographs, we are grateful to Bellini Juvenile Designer Furniture, Susan Bortolotto, Kids' Designs, Larry's Baby Safety Services, Lullaby Lane, Nu-line Industries, and Steve's Sport Shop.

We also express appreciation to Barbara Armentrout and Fran Feldman for editing the manuscript.

Developmental Editor
Susan Warton

Coordinating Editor
Deborah Thomas Kramer

Design
Kathy Avanzino Barone

Illustrations
Barbara Tapp
Rik Olson

Photo Stylist
JoAnn Masaoka

Photographers: Richard Fish: 31 top; **Pamela Harper:** 46; **Stephen Marley:** 2, 13, 21, 22 left, 27, 30, 32, 47, 59, 61, 65, 66, 67, 69, 74, 77; **Jack McDowell:** 41, 49 top; **Darrow Watt:** 31 right, 39 right, 44, 45; **Tom Wyatt:** 17, 22 right, 31 left, 39 left, 42, 49 bottom.

Cover: His lovable innocence can quickly get him into trouble unless mom, dad, and a safety gate protect him from harm. Photography by Darrow M. Watt. Photo styling by JoAnn Masaoka.

Sunset Books
  Editor: David E. Clark
  Managing Editor: Elizabeth L. Hogan

First printing January 1988

Contents

Special Features

Bundles of Joy

How to keep your children safe

The very young are both innocent and curious, a combination that makes them especially vulnerable to accidents. A shiny penny looks good enough to taste. A wall outlet looks intriguing to probe. The neighbor's dog resembles a big, furry toy.

Maybe the staircase challenges children to climb before they are quite ready, or the open front door beckons them to dart outside. The reason the early years are so accident-prone is that young children are growing at such a fast clip, bursting with energy as they go.

As you chase your little bundle of energy around the house, be aware that there's plenty you can do to make his or her world safer. *Making Your Home Child-Safe* points the way. Besides the primary objective of preventing accidents, a child-safe home can also give parents greater peace of mind, as well as more time to sit down and catch their breath.

Safety pays off

In today's world of medical miracles, most diseases that once took children's lives have been brought under control. Many have disappeared from public awareness. Today, accidents in the home claim more children's lives than all childhood diseases combined.

A perfectly accident-free environment is too much to hope for. The most capable and conscientious parents in the world could not completely eliminate all dangers. And probably we all need a few mishaps to help us learn. If parents become too zealous about accident prevention, it can stifle a child's spirit.

But it's also good to keep in mind that accidents don't just happen. Something always causes them. With a thoughtful approach and the help of this book, risks of severe harm to your child can be minimized. Think of this book as your partner in childproofing. You provide the understanding of your son or daughter, an awareness of your home environment, and common sense. Let the book contribute planning tips, creative ideas, and practical answers.

Using this book

Arranged in four main chapters, *Making Your Home Child-Safe* first takes you on a childproofing "tour" through the house—room by room. Next, it goes outdoors to the play yard, pool, and other outside areas. Then it examines typical baby equipment, pointing out safety features and potential hazards from misuse.

Finally, the book presents general safety advice valuable to any family—from how to be prepared in advance in case of fire to arranging babysitting so that you can leave with confidence for an evening.

What to expect

Psychologists have compared a parent's role to that of an athletic coach. In the case of young children, "lifeguard" is sometimes a more appropriate job description. Early childhood is a period for parents to be especially vigilant as their little ones constantly grab, topple, climb, taste, and get into everything they can find.

Anticipation. Basic to keeping small children safe is knowing generally what to expect with each stage of growth. Even so, you'll often be surprised. But an awareness of your youngster's developing skills can help you to avert accidents. For example, you'll need to remove bumper pads from the crib before your baby figures out how to use them as a boost to climbing out.

Individual differences. Like the rest of us, little children are individuals with a wide range in rates of development. Some talk early, some walk early. Some are adventurous, some more cautious.

Wriggler

Some are agile, some more awkward. Some kids just seem to be naturally accident-prone, while others steer clear of trouble.

Who gets hurt? At certain ages, such as from about 18 months to 2½ years, children have more accidents, simply because they're increasingly active without much understanding of danger. If you say "no" at these early ages, they may learn what you mean, but they won't remember it for long.

Generally, daring, aggressive kids get into more mischief than timid or reserved kids. Accidents are more likely to happen, too, when a child is under stress—at someone else's house, during an exciting event, or at a party. Watch out when your son or daughter is tired, hungry, or frustrated, or when there's any strain or instability at home.

Stages of early growth

Curiosity is the essence of learning; it's also a universal human trait. Babies seem to have more than their share. From the moment they're introduced to this complex and interesting world, they start their quest for information. Everything around them is new and fascinating, eagerly seen, heard, touched, tasted, sniffed, or chewed.

As babies develop the skills of reaching and grasping, then moving about, both their ability to gather more information and their potential for accidents take a giant leap forward.

Wrigglers. During the first three months of life, newborn babies lack the mobility to get into much trouble. They reach out, wriggle, smile, cry, eat, fill diapers, and wake their parents. They arch

their backs and dig in their heels. Most movements are reflex actions, but they can be enough to carry an infant off a changing table or a bed if you're not standing protectively by.

Babies who've never rolled over can do so quickly and unexpectedly. Most accidents at this age can be prevented if parents understand infancy and the protective care infants demand.

By the third or fourth month, wriggling babies can hold their heads upright, as well as grasp things and get them into their mouths. Make sure that whatever goes into baby's mouth won't cause choking.

Creepers and crawlers. Sometimes as early as the fifth month, babies start moving around. At 6 or 7 months, babies learn to sit up on their own. They pick things up more carefully, between thumb and forefinger, and study them. They like to drop things, too. You can tell that they are developing memories and starting to learn from experience.

As mobility increases—often faster than you expect—babies creep, crawl, and eventually walk. Each has an individual

Crawler

style of locomotion; a few choose not to creep at all, just to walk when they're ready.

This new mobility signals the time to make sure that your entire house is baby-safe. On any day, your crawler may open a cabinet or find an electrical outlet. New physical efforts lead babies to pull things over on themselves, and to fall down a lot.

Fascination with tasting continues and babies keep putting everything possible into their mouths. Keep a sharp eye out for small items on the floor or low surfaces, and pick them up.

During this period, baby's first tooth will probably arrive and, with it, an urge to chew. Make sure that extension cords and other objects that look chewable are kept out of reach.

Walkers. In the last part of the first year, activity becomes more constant. After scooting and crawling everywhere, babies usually start walking sometime around their first birthday.

But the child still can't perceive danger with much realism. Mobility is not balanced with good judgment. Your job now will be to encourage baby's exploration and thirst to learn, while providing the safest possible context. The idea is to protect without stifling or scaring.

Look around your house with a fresh eye, making sure that it's as safe for your child now as it was earlier. Check that any doors leading to dangerous areas remain closed, either by locking them or using doorknob sleeves (see page 35). Baby can now get into almost everything within reach.

As baby starts walking, many parents start teaching the meaning of *no* for the first time. Most child guidance experts agree that, to be effective, *no* should be used sparingly, consistently, and mainly when children's activities endanger themselves, others, or valued objects.

But don't rely on *no* as your sole safeguard at this point. Be ready to follow it up by calmly but firmly removing either the object or the child. And don't expect a young toddler to remember *no* for very long after you say it.

Explorers. Armed with mobility and more than enough energy for the whole family, a toddler starts testing independence in the second year, as well as trying out all kinds of new behaviors and skills.

These little explorers work daily to refine their walking, talking, and visual perception. They learn to climb on tables and up bookcases. They race from one activity to another, experimenting with whatever they can lay their hands on, from tap water to cat food.

Be sure that at this stage, your house and yard are as child-safe as you can make them. Protect anything that you value, too.

As ages 2 and 3 roll around, children become full-fledged explorers eager to get into everything. They still have only a limited awareness of danger. Though they may understand simple rules, you can't count on them to mind, or to remember. At this age, most parents use gentle discipline to set limits.

Continue to keep a watchful eye on your little ones as they grow and to provide a safe environment for them. Safety should always be a basic family concern, regardless of the age of your children.

Walker

Explorer

Home, Safe Home

Childproofing your house

By the time we reach parenthood, most of us have become pretty nonchalant about the worlds of stimuli around us. But imagine the wonder of a baby for whom every object is brand new—something fascinating to look at, pick up, test, taste, and chew. Colors, shapes, textures, smells—all receive a baby's eager attention.

Throughout your child's early growth, it's your job to provide a safe environment, along with experiences that will encourage learning. Because the very young lack understanding of dangers, adults must protect them from hazards and steer them to safe situations, objects, and behavior patterns.

Any house is full of fascination to a small child. It's also full of hazards: household chemicals, electrical outlets, objects small enough to go into the mouth, and many others. In this chapter, you will learn how to spot these dangers and eliminate, reduce, or block them off.

The idea is to "build in" as much home safety as possible. Though safety can never be absolute, much can be done to prevent accidents at home. There are other benefits to a child-safe home, too: by establishing safety measures and safe habits, parents can free their time and energy for greater enjoyment of their children—and can cut back on the need to say "no."

To be prepared for each stage of growth, it helps to childproof your house completely from the outset, even before your child's birth. If you babyproof only for your baby's present skill level, no sooner will you have "crawlproofed" your house than your little one will be off and walking.

What to Do Right Away

Childproofing throughout the house is important, but accident statistics show that some jobs are more urgent than others. Here are a few top-priority tasks that will make your home much safer in just a few minutes. After you've completed these steps, the rest of this chapter will guide you to room-by-room childproofing.

Emergency numbers

On a separate card for each phone in the house, write down the numbers for the following; post a card on or adjacent to every phone where all family members and the babysitter can find it.

■ Police, fire department, ambulance (in many areas, 911 will connect you with all of these; if the 911 number is not in operation in your area, dial "O" for operator)

■ Poison control center

■ Family physician or pediatrician

■ Health plan medical number

■ Any other numbers that might be important, such as those of parents' work, neighbors, relatives, and friends

For an even more complete listing, fill in the emergency information on the inside back cover of this book.

Pick up...

Comb floor surfaces and furniture for anything that is tiny enough to fit into a baby's mouth or that might be otherwise dangerous. First, thoroughly vacuum carpets and floors. Next, get down on your hands and knees and survey from your baby's point of view. You may be amazed at the pins, buttons, coins, bits of string, and stray peanuts that have lodged under furniture and in deep-pile carpeting.

...& lock up

Store well out of a child's reach, or lock up, all household supplies that could be toxic, such as
■ detergents and cleaning agents (including drain, oven, and toilet-bowl cleaners) ■ disinfectants and deodorizers (use only non-toxic diaper-pail deodorants) ■ polishes (for shoes, floors, furniture) ■ plant-care chemicals ■ tobacco products (including matches, lighters, and lighter fluid) ■ pesticides (such as ant or roach poison, flea powder, moth balls) ■ petroleum distillates (such as kerosene, turpentine, automotive products; always store in metal containers) ■ pharmaceuticals (even vitamins can be dangerous) ■ art and hobby supplies that contain harmful ingredients.

Be sure that all medications you buy have child-resistant caps. But don't trust the package design alone: yours may be the one child in a thousand who can figure it out. Keep these items well out of reach or locked up.

Also, *always read labels carefully*—but be aware that, although some poisonous substances are clearly marked, many are not. Make sure that all toxics you store are correctly labeled with name and ingredients. This information can save a life by letting the doctor or poison control

Outlet caps *cover electrical outlets, preventing children from inserting objects. (Eventually, though, some kids may learn to pull caps off.)*

Spring-loaded *offset cover plates block direct access to outlets. To insert a plug, twist ¼ turn clockwise until holes in plate and outlet line up.*

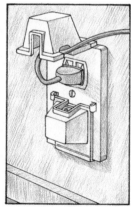

Protective covers *over outlets prevent accidental shocks. Covers flip out of the way for insertion or removal of a plug.*

center know what antidote and treatment to use in the event of poisoning.

Keep a small bottle of *syrup of ipecac* with your first-aid supplies, to induce vomiting after baby has swallowed a hazardous substance if directed by the doctor or poison control center. Never induce vomiting until so directed, because vomiting a caustic or petroleum-based product (such as furniture polish) could increase the internal harm.

To be safest, simply get rid of the worst poisons unless you absolutely need them.

Other safeguards

By making a few simple changes in your home, you can make it a safer place for everyone.

Electrical cords must be kept out of reach. A baby can receive severe electrical burns and permanent scars from chewing on them or may topple a heavy appliance by tugging on them. Worn, cloth-covered cords are especially dangerous, so replace them with up-to-date rugged plastic cords.

Eliminate extension cords wherever possible by rearranging furniture. If you must use an extension cord, unplug it when not in use.

Also cover electrical outlets. Although young children can remove outlet caps (see facing page), caps do discourage them from inserting objects into unused outlets. Put covers on all outlets.

Doorknob sleeves (see page 35) can safeguard doors that you want to keep closed.

Smoke detectors should be installed and maintained as directed on page 73.

CHILDPROOF LATCHES & LOCKS

Little curiosity-seekers love to open cabinets and drawers and search for mysterious and interesting finds. In the occasional cabinet or drawer that contains nothing but child-safe items, such exploring is harmless. But most cabinets and drawers are where adults usu-ally stash all the dangerous things little explorers should not get into.

This page shows several child-resistant latches and locks. All are easy to install; follow the manufacturer's recommendations.

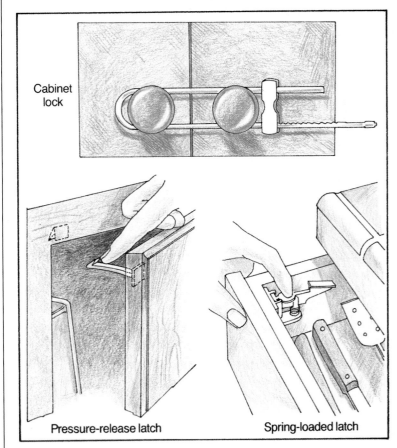

Cabinet lock

Pressure-release latch

Spring-loaded latch

Childproof latches and locks keep babies and toddlers from opening drawers and cabinet doors (or double doors to closets or rooms). The simple plastic devices are easily opened by adults but are beyond the skills and strength of young children. Eventually, though, some kids may learn how to get past these restraints.

Kitchen Safety

In many homes, the kitchen is the bustling hub of family life, where kids and adults are together daily. As a rule, moms and dads spend considerable time there preparing for and cleaning up after meals.

But the kitchen is not a safe place for a young child to be underfoot. From its hot foods to its sharp knives, the kitchen is your home's most accident-prone area for small family members.

Baby's own cabinet

To keep baby out of harm's way, make one lower kitchen cabinet or drawer baby's own kitchen space, away from your work center yet within view. In it, store plastic or metal bowls, containers, a colander, measuring cups, and other safe, unbreakable cookware for play. Or park a playpen or feeding table in a safe spot, so that you and baby can see each other and chat.

Other cabinets & drawers

Because your young son or daughter is sure to wander alone into the kitchen from time to time, you'll want to clean out any cabinets within the child's reach that contain dangerous items. In most kitchens, the place to start is under the sink.

Move frequently used supplies, such as dishwasher detergent, to an upper cabinet with an easy-access latch (see page 11). Put garbage in a container with a hard-to-open lid—or store it under the sink and install a child-resistant latch on that door.

Most kitchen cleansers and related chemicals are packaged in bright containers that make them look edible or drinkable to a small, curious child. So don't leave any of these products within reach. And never store them in containers that originally held food or drink, such as soft-drink bottles.

Move liquor to a cabinet with a child-resistant latch or to an out-of-reach spot. Also keep knives safely beyond your child's reach—yet convenient to you, so that you'll be sure to put them away again after use.

Find a new place to keep aluminum foil and other wraps boxed with sharp cutting edges, so that your child won't discover them.

Safer countertops

Don't let any electrical cords dangle over countertop edges where they might be pulled.

Put away all kitchen utensils after use. Small appliances such as mixers, food processors, coffee-makers, and the like should be unplugged when not in use and stored out of reach. Always remove and put away any sharp blades. Appliances or

In the kitchen, *a playpen or feeding table set a safe distance from the range and other hazards protects baby while allowing companionship with mom. Pot handles are turned inward to prevent spills, and railing (from children's store) guards against burns. Design: Lizette Wilbur.*

bowls too close to the edge of the counter can be pulled down by inquisitive little hands.

To be ideally safe, low countertops should have curved corners and edges rather than sharp, protruding ones that could hurt heads. On sharp-edged counters, you can install corner guards (see below).

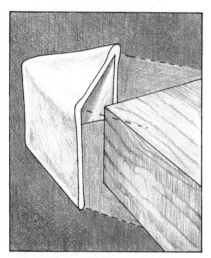

Corner guards of soft plastic protect against injury if a child accidentally bumps against a counter or tabletop.

Kitchen appliances

As manufacturers respond to public concern and family needs, many major appliances are now available with child-safe features. When buying new appliances, look for models with switches and knobs beyond a small child's reach.

Here are other pointers, whether your appliances are brand new or long used.

Refrigerator. Some foods found in refrigerators can be toxic to children, especially if taken in quantity; examples are wine, picante sauce, and spoiled leftovers. (Check for and discard spoiled and unwanted foods routinely.)

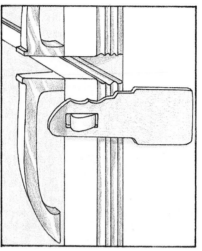

To foil small snackers, just lock the refrigerator with a plastic device sold in children's stores. Do not use it on an empty or unused refrigerator.

To prevent children from opening the refrigerator door, you can install a refrigerator lock (see above) at the top of the door. But very young children usually lack the strength and coordination to open a refrigerator door. And when they're able to do so, they're also old enough to be taught that the refrigerator is off limits. In the long run, saying "no" is a more helpful safeguard than using a lock. (Also see page 41 about the hazard of stored, empty refrigerators.)

Trash compactor. A trash compactor is handy for squeezing a lot of garbage into a small bag. If your kitchen has a trash compactor, be sure it won't operate when the door is open and that it can be turned on only with a key. Put the key where your child can't get it.

Garbage disposer. If your child can reach the garbage disposer switch, there are a couple of methods to keep him or her from flipping it on. Replace the cover plate with a locking outdoor switch cover or replace the switch with a key-switch (like the ones used for lights at schools). Both of these are available at electrical supply shops.

Dishwasher. Kids love to push buttons, so most dishwasher control panels are irresistible. Obviously, the easiest way to keep your child from playing with the dishwasher's controls or contents is to buy a dishwasher that is difficult for a child to operate and open. But, if you're not in the market for a new dishwasher, you can slow down your child's exploration by locking the dishwasher door with an appliance fastener available where child safety supplies are sold. (Because the locking device may be within your child's reach, it won't be entirely childproof.)

Load knives and sharp objects pointing downward so they are not as hazardous when the door is open. Pour in dish-

As a safety precaution, make it a habit to point knife blades down when loading the dishwasher. Unload sharp and breakable items promptly after washing.

washing detergent just before you run the dishwasher; many detergents are toxic if swallowed.

Cooktop and oven. Teach your child at an early age the meaning of "hot"—and that the stove, whether on or off, is a "no-no."

Make sure that he or she is not underfoot when you are working at a cooktop, oven, or other appliance with hot foods or grease that might spill or spatter. When cooking, keep pot handles turned inward (but not over another burner) so small children can't reach them. The stove-top guard shown on page 13 provides a barricade—but don't consider it a guarantee of safety. And don't leave hot pots, pans, or appliances where a toddler might climb to them.

If the door or outer walls of the oven get hot to the touch, keep baby away from them. And if your toddler can reach the controls, see if you can remove the knobs; keep them nearby until this activity is forgotten.

If an accident happens in spite of your precautions, *immediately immerse the burned area in a stream of cold water until the pain subsides.* (Don't use ice, which may cause frostbite.) Then cover the burn loosely with a clean bandage and call your child's doctor. (Turn to page 72 for general fire safety information.)

Baby's own drawer, filled with lightweight plastic or metal pots and utensils, provides plenty to play with while keeping mom company in the kitchen.

Microwave oven. Be sure the microwave oven is mounted where baby can't reach the controls.

The microwave oven is very convenient for busy families. But *a word of caution:* if you use it to heat baby food or baby bottles, the containers may not feel hot even when the food is scalding. Tiny mouths have been burned by overly heated foods from microwave ovens. Be sure to heed manufacturer's instructions.

After heating a bottle (with nipple on), shake or mix well and test the temperature of the milk or formula on the inside of your wrist. When heating baby food, always stir and, again, check the temperature on your wrist before giving the food to your child. (Use these precautions when heating food conventionally, too.)

Other kitchen childproofing

Consider replacing the kitchen's ordinary receptacles with GFCI-protected (ground fault circuit interrupter) receptacles—or installing GFCI breakers at the panel box in place of ordinary circuit breakers (see page 19). These steps will guard against the hazard of serious electrical shock.

For flooring, choose resilient, textured material that resists slips, softens impact, and wipes clean easily. Such floors are also relatively quiet under clattering feet.

If you use refrigerator magnets, make sure they are too big to go into a small child's mouth and that the magnet itself can't come loose. Otherwise, put these away for a few years.

Bathroom Safety

Medicines that look or taste like candy, slippery tubs and floors, very hot water—these are some of the hazards that bathrooms present to curious young children. Here are steps you can take to make your home's bathrooms as safe as possible.

Reorganize your medicine cabinets

First, empty everything out of the medicine cabinets. Then reorganize. Flush down the toilet any outdated or unneeded medications or any that have changed noticeably in odor or color. Also get rid of perfumes, lotions, ointments, cosmetics, and powders you don't use and wouldn't want your toddler to ingest.

Put out of reach. Put on the highest shelves those dangerous items you choose to keep (make sure, though, that your child can't climb up to them)—or, even better, in a locked cabinet. If you have a standard, wall-mounted medicine cabinet that doesn't lock, add a safety lock like the one shown above at right. Or store the items in a lockable tool box, fishing tackle box, or small overnight suitcase.

Tidy up. Keep razors, perfumes, medications, powders, creams,

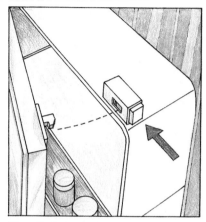

Keep little explorers out of the medicine cabinet with this self-adhesive plastic latch. To open, mom or dad simply presses the button shown by the arrow—easy for grownups, but impossible for a small child.

and cosmetics off the counter—or anywhere else that a small child might find them. Never allow your baby to play with empty medicine containers, because full ones might then be mistaken for toys. Wrap up used disposable razors and razor blades and place them in outdoor trash cans.

Childproof other cabinets

Go through all bathroom drawers and cabinets from the vantage point of a young child. Clear away cleansers, pins and other sharp objects, and all other potential poisons and hazards. Install door and drawer latches, such as those shown on page 11. In places that your child can

reach (or could conceivably climb to), store only harmless items, such as towels.

Bathtub safety

Tragically, some children drown in the bathtub, so this is an area for strict supervision. Also, burns from scalding water are a common, yet preventable, accident when bathing small children.

Pay constant attention. When bathing an infant, always use one hand to support the baby.

Never leave your infant or young child during a bath—not even for an instant. If you must answer the door or telephone, wrap your baby in a towel and take him or her with you. Drownings can occur in just one or two inches of water.

Not too hot! Reduce the risk of a severe tap-water burn by taking one simple step: adjust the thermostat on your water heater so that your tap water is no more than 120°F. (This is hot enough for washing dishes and laundry.)

About an hour after turning down the water heater's thermostat, measure the tap water temperature by placing a cooking thermometer in a glass; run hot water over it for a couple of minutes and then read the tempera-

Bathing is usually great fun. *To make sure it's also safe, gently support your child with one hand—and don't leave, even for a moment. Fill the tub with comfortably warm water. A spout guard over the faucet safeguards against bumps.*

...bathroom safety

ture. You may need to adjust the thermostat dial slightly and test again. When the temperature is right, mark the new, safe level on the thermostat as shown at right. This will let you know if the thermostat is turned accidentally.

You can also double-check the water's temperature with a bathtub thermometer, available at most children's stores. But you don't really need one; just feel the water with your elbow (not your hand, which is less sensitive). Fill a baby's bath with cool water first; then add warm. Finish with a little cold water to cool off the spout. Check that the water is comfortably warm, about 90°F.

Adjust the thermostat on your water heater so tap water gets no hotter than 120°F; mark the setting.

Baby's tub

For bathing a baby, use a steady, stable, baby-sized tub either inside the main tub or set on a wide, sturdy counter. There are also freestanding tubs. Or, while your baby is still small enough, you might prefer the kitchen sink. For nestling baby comfortably on a hard tub or sink, purchase a special baby-sized sponge mat or use a folded towel.

Toddler's tub. After your child outgrows the infant tub, provide a rubberized mat, bathtub friction decals (shown below), or nonslip tape in the main bathtub to prevent slipping. Or, for kids from about 6 months to 2½ years old, a special suction-cupped baby support (see below at left) is available at children's stores. Here, you can also find protectors, such as the one illustrated on page 17, to cover the tub spout to minimize head bumps and burns.

Rows of adhesive decals do more than just decorate the bathtub; they also make the tub less slippery.

Unsafe tubs. Sunken and extra-deep bathtubs present more than the usual hazard. The closer the tub's rim to the floor, the more easily a child can climb it and tumble in. If your bathroom has a low-rimmed tub, be sure to keep the bathroom door closed.

Plastic support with suction cups and soft foam cushion seat holds a wriggling 9-month-old baby securely in tub. (Even so, never leave a child alone in the bath.)

Don't bathe your baby in the shower, because the water can unexpectedly or accidentally become scalding hot. And if your shower or tub has a glass door, it must be safety glass to guard against injury on the day your child decides to pound it with something heavy.

Be cautious about bathing a child in a spa-type bathtub. Children under 3 often can't support themselves in the swirling water. If you have this type of tub, don't run the pump during your young child's bath.

Avoiding shock

Cap or cover bathroom outlets. Because of its moisture, the bathroom poses greater electrical hazards for everyone than any other room in the house. Bathroom outlets should be protected by a ground fault circuit interrupter (GFCI) to prevent serious shock. You can buy GFCI replacement receptacles at building or electrical supply stores (see above).

It's safest to keep radios, hair dryers, curling irons, and other electrical appliances out of the bathroom during your child's early years. If there are some that you consider essential to your comfort, take precautions with them. Unplug them when you're not using them. Let hot appliances cool off well out of your child's reach. And keep all electrical appliances a safe distance from the bathtub and sink as a safeguard against electrocution. For the same reason, *never use extension cords or a portable heater in the bathroom.*

Other safety checks

If you've been using automatic toilet-bowl cleaner, remove it from the tank and discard it in the outside trash; such products are toxic.

GFCIs: A GOOD IDEA

Since 1984, the Uniform Building Code has required ground fault circuit interrupters in bathrooms; more recently, they've been required for kitchens and outdoor circuits, too. The reasoning is that these are the likeliest areas where serious electrical shock could occur, a hazard that's greater near water.

GFCI-protected receptacles are a good idea, whether you're putting in new receptacles or changing existing ones. The GFCI receptacle senses a leak in the current and breaks the circuit almost instantaneously, thus preventing electrical shock. If wired correctly in line, one unit can serve several receptacles. Or, you can replace ordinary circuit breakers that serve your kitchen, bath, and outdoor receptacles with GFCI breakers.

Sunset's Basic Home Wiring explains how to wire your own GFCI. Otherwise, hire a licensed electrician. Manufacturers recommend checking the devices by triggering the test button monthly.

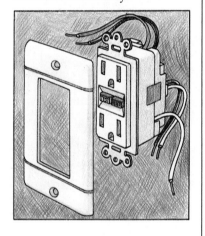

To keep the lid down so your toddler can't explore the toilet bowl, you can buy a simple self-gripping strap from a baby store.

For the first stage of toilet training, use a "potty chair" that sits on the floor. Then, when your child is ready, move to a step-up training seat that lets him or her use the adult toilet safely. Or you can get a two-stage toilet trainer that does both. Choose a sturdy step-up trainer with a nonslip step and handles to assure that your child can get up and down safely.

Look at the location of the towel bars from a toddler's vantage point. Could they be used as handrails by a climbing child? Could they poke a small face?

Hide the wastebasket inside a safety-latched cabinet. You can purchase lid-locking diaper pails, a design so practical that you may wish to use a second one as a wastebasket. Check the laundry chute or hamper to be sure that baby can't get trapped in it or fall through it.

Make sure that bathroom doors can be unlocked from the outside in case your child locks one from within. If necessary, change the locks.

Certain kinds of tile and linoleum bathroom floors can be very slippery whether they're wet or dry. If yours presents this hazard, lay down a rubber-backed bath mat.

Even after your bathroom passes all the safety checks, however, it still won't be a safe enough place for your child to play there alone.

Baby's Nursery

As you would all other rooms in the house, start babyproofing the nursery by studying it from an infant's point of view. Even if your tiny son or daughter doesn't yet crawl, it won't be long before he or she does. So, clear the way for safer explorations by eliminating any hazards now.

■ Are there small objects on the floor or within a baby's reach that could find their way into a crawling baby's mouth?

■ Are there electrical cords or uncovered outlets within reach of a curious baby? (See page 10 for ways to block these.)

■ Could little fingers or feet get burned by touching an unguarded heating register, radiator, or other heat source? (To screen these off, see page 29.)

■ Are there any plants, filmy plastic (such as dry cleaning bags), household cleansers, medications, or other potentially dangerous items in the nursery?

■ Are baby care products kept well beyond the tot's reach? Is the diaper pail impossible for him or her to open?

■ Are crib and playpen placed far enough away from windows to keep your baby out of hot sunlight and drafts (or—a little later—to keep your toddler from accidentally pulling down drapes, breaking the window pane, or even climbing out the window)?

■ Is there a dangling cord from a heater, fan, lamp, or other appliance within your baby's reach from crib, playpen, changing table, or floor? If so, either remove these things or rearrange the room to block access to them.

■ Do nursery shades, draperies, or blinds have long cords? If so, cut them off or adjust them to their shortest possible lengths and eliminate loops. If you need to keep the cord long, wrap it around a screwed-on cleat high on the wall, out of baby's reach. (Small children can strangle themselves accidentally with cords.)

Crib accessories

Check crib toys and clothing for ribbons, strings, or cords, and remove them. Even a mobile should be hung where it can't fall into the crib or be reached by your growing baby. Other innocent-looking hazards are cords of toy telephones and necklaces. Never run a cord through a pacifier.

Reading a book is one of many activities, besides sleeping, that a baby enjoys in a safe and comfortable nursery.

Remove crib toys strung across the crib (or playpen) when your baby begins to push up on its hands and knees or at 5 months of age.

Beware that pillows can suffocate a baby. And never cover mattresses or pillows with plastic film for the same reason. Another safeguard: Do not prop a bottle at feeding time; instead, hold baby and bottle yourself.

For complete information on safe beds for babies, see page 56.

At the changing table

At some point, and probably sooner than you expect, your baby will suddenly turn over. To safeguard against a fall, the changing table needs fenced sides, as well as a safety strap. Even with these precautions, however, never leave your baby there unattended—don't underestimate his or her power to wriggle or roll.

Keep sharp objects, small items, medications, powders, and creams well out of your baby's reach. Always close canisters of powder after use: a cloud of fine dust could choke the baby or cause pneumonia.

Put disposable and used diapers, as well as the diaper pail, where your child can't reach them. Cake deodorants for the diaper pail are sometimes toxic— and tempting to a small explorer. You can purchase diaper pails with childproof lids, as well as nontoxic deodorants.

For a safe environment

First of all, if you haven't yet done so, install a smoke detector just outside the nursery (see page 75).

Next, make absolutely sure that neither your child's room (nor any other room in the house) nor its furnishings or toys are painted with lead-based or otherwise toxic finishes. This danger could be present if exterior paint was used on anything in the room or if any furniture is a hand-me-down or an antique (safety regulation of lead paint became effective in 1978). Remove any suspect paint completely before repainting with a nontoxic paint. Keep the baby out of the room during the stripping and repainting process, well away from the dust, chips, vapors, and fumes.

Investigate friendly and practical materials for wall and floor surfaces (page 25) before you do any redecorating.

For convenience, you may want to consider buying a simple intercom that lets you listen to baby during nap-time or at night when you are elsewhere in the house.

Awake or asleep, *a baby spends considerable time in the nursery. Keep surroundings soft, peaceful, and safe for a happy start in life.*

Toddler's Room & Furnishings

When your baby stands up and takes off one day—look out! With a toddler's mobility, the world is soon at his or her fingertips.

Because toddlers spend many hours in their rooms playing, stacking, climbing, chattering, learning, laughing, and sleeping, you'll want to make these places as safe as possible. It won't stop every fall or accident, but it will reduce chances of serious harm.

Climbing & falling

Take the same safety precautions as outlined for infants (see page 20). But also consider a toddler's expanding skills. Most toddlers, for example, will try to climb almost anything, and many will succeed. So, arrange furniture to make sure your child won't climb to dangerous heights. Place no climbable objects under windows.

Now is the time when you'll appreciate a cushioning floor covering. Besides softening falls, it cuts down on toddler noise. Choose durable carpeting; throw rugs cause too many skids and falls.

An active child may wreak havoc on all surfaces of the room. But you can provide easy-care, protective paints and other finishes (see page 25 for suggestions for floors and walls).

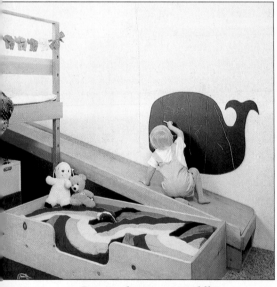

For an adventurous toddler, these furnishings provide climbing experiences within safe limits. Design: Don Vandervort.

Pint-sized furniture has rounded edges to safeguard against bumps. Covered with plastic laminate, bed and chest are easily wiped clean; bed has a guardrail.

Safe furniture

If your child stands taller than 35 inches or can climb out of the crib, even with its gate up, it's time to graduate to a standard bed.

Sleeping safely. The bed is often safest in a corner, fenced by walls on two sides. If it measures more than a foot off the floor, a low guardrail along the open side will help prevent injuries from falls. Make sure that the space between the rail and bed frame will not allow a small child to slip or wiggle through. Bunkbeds present the risk of falling at any age and are not recommended for toddlers.

A simpler and often safer option is a Japanese *futon* (a long, folding cushion) or a firm mattress laid on a carpeted floor.

For toddlers, the best bed frames have very simple headboards and footboards free of decorative cutouts or protrusions that might catch or poke.

Electric blankets are best saved for adult use.

Storage ideas. Save low drawers and shelves for toys and bulky items. Use upper drawers and shelves that are out of your toddler's reach for potentially messy items, such as art supplies. Store fragile baby treasures and all dangerous articles (such as safety pins, scissors, lotions, medications, or objects small enough to swallow) in high, safety-latched cupboards (see page 11) in a different room.

If you're choosing a traditional toy chest, look for a spring-loaded support that prevents the lid from slamming shut, as well as construction that prevents the hinge sides from pinching little fingers. It should also have ventilation holes in the base. Safer choices for toy storage are plastic tubs or bins or low, sturdy shelves. Cardboard boxes are good, too, and are easily replaced.

Choosing chairs and tables. Be sure stools, chairs, and tables are quite stable, because your child will climb on them, invent many new uses for them, and maybe stack them up, too.

If buying new furniture, opt for child-sized pieces: adult sizes are less comfortable for kids—and less safe for the very young. Durable materials, softness, rounded edges, stability, and adjustability are features to look for in children's furniture.

Check the baby gear information beginning on page 54. Childproof windows and doors in your toddler's room (see pages 34–35). Be sure that there are no closet hooks at eye level. And provide a night-light so both you and your child can find your way through the room at night. An overhead fixture is generally safer than a table lamp. Floor lamps may look like play equipment and can tip over easily.

Tape electrical cords to baseboards, using 2-inch-wide clear packing tape (run it along the cord's length), or simply block access to the cords with furniture.

Stacking baskets of lightweight plastic provide safe and practical storage for a toddler's toys.

Bedrooms & Closets

Inspect all family bedrooms and closets for hazards. As in all rooms, keep floors thoroughly vacuumed. Put away throw rugs, since small children can skid or trip on them easily.

Even after the inspection, don't let baby play alone in these areas. Close doors and—if necessary—add doorknob sleeves (see page 35).

Brothers' & sisters' rooms

Many older brothers and sisters will gladly help you keep baby out of their personal domain—they know the damage that could occur otherwise.

Make sure that doors stay shut, especially during school hours. Allow your baby or toddler to visit these spaces only by invitation.

Master bedroom

Clear the tops of bedstands of medications and objects that are small enough to fit into baby's mouth or are otherwise dangerous. Keep a sharp eye out for earrings, tie pins, cotton balls, pills, buttons, safety pins, paper clips, and coins.

Lock up hazards. If you must keep medications or other hazardous items at bedside, put them in a locked drawer. Otherwise, lock them in a bathroom medicine cabinet or keep them in a separate locked box. Also lock up matches, cigarettes, ashtrays, lighters, pipes, tobacco, and incense—or keep them all well out of reach.

Check dresser and cabinet tops for perfume, cosmetics, jewelry, medications, and other sharp, poisonous, or tiny objects. Lock anything dangerous in a drawer or behind doors that are safety latched. Your dresser top may look too high for little fingers to reach, but where there's a will, toddlers usually find a way. To

Dressing up in borrowed finery is one of the big attractions of visiting mom's or dad's closet.

divert your child, you may want to reserve a bottom drawer for your youngster, as we suggest for the kitchen on page 12. Fill it with interesting but safe articles and dress-up clothes.

Out of sight, out of mind. Place furniture so that it hides electrical cords. Tie up any dangling shade or curtain cords. After vacuuming, get down on your hands and knees to scan the floor for small objects (don't forget to look under the bed and other furnishings). Put the wastebasket out of reach or inside a safety-latched cabinet. Remove house plants, or hang them securely out of reach. Also find high perches for breakable ornaments.

A clean, safe closet

Check the bedroom closet for small or dangerous items. Place jewelry and other delicate items in containers beyond reach on upper closet shelves or in hanging closet-storage containers that zip shut (toward the top). Be sure that any closet hooks, including ones on the door, are placed well above a child's eye level. Remove plastic dry cleaner's bags, tie them in knots, and discard them in the outside trash. Lock up shoe polish, moth balls, camphor, and any other dangerous products or dispose of them in the outdoor trash can.

Be aware that young children sometimes like to hide in closets or chests. Be sure your child can't get trapped inside accidentally.

CHILD-FRIENDLY SURFACES

Sticky fingers, smeared crayons, spattering orange juice—with a small child around, your house is bound to receive plenty of colorful wear and tear. Some wall- and floor-covering materials are more durable, easier to clean, and safer than others.

Washable walls

If wall coverings are durable and easy to clean, they'll continue over time to look as good below the 3-foot level (where children can reach) as they do above it.

Paints. Nontoxic, water-based acrylic paint offers a low-luster finish, washability, and chip resistance. For trim and areas that receive considerable wear, choose a nontoxic, water-based, semigloss enamel. (Glossy finishes are easier to clean, but every nick or bump is highlighted by their sheen.) Buy high-quality paints and choose neutral colors (they'll smudge least).

Wallpapers. As children discover crayons and paint, sometimes they can't resist a little scribbling or dabbling on the wall. One of

the easiest-to-wash wall coverings is fabric-backed vinyl. Other relatively durable choices include solid vinyl and vinyl-coated wallpaper. Woven-fabric plastic coverings are also excellent choices for durability. All sponge off easily. Random or free-flowing patterns help hide dirt and damage.

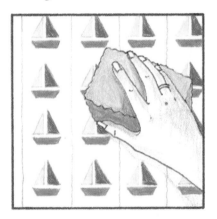

Other wall materials. Some children's room designers opt for industrial carpeting on one or more walls. It's rugged and easy to clean (just vacuum); it also cuts down on noise and provides a padded, soft surface.

Flooring

When choosing new flooring with children in mind, decide whether the room or area will need a hard floor covering or soft carpeting.

Carpeting. This is the friendliest choice for nursery, family room, living room, hallway, and stairs —wherever comfort, safety, and sound absorption are important. Because it can be damaged by moisture and spills, carpeting is less practical in kitchens, bath-

rooms, and dining areas.

Because of its wearability and commercial grade, 100 percent nylon carpeting is a good choice for kids. Nylon carpets tend to be more stain resistant than wool ones, as well as less expensive to buy and keep clean. If treated with a stain repellent, spills will be even easier to wipe up. Most nylon carpets have a built-in static guard. By law, all carpets are fire retardant.

Pick low cut-pile or short-loop, dense-weave carpets. Don't choose deep shags, which might conceal dangerous small objects. Choose a mid-range color— neither too dark nor too light. A variegated texture or pattern will camouflage stains.

Carpet tiles are another good option for floors, though somewhat expensive. You can install them yourself; if one section gets stained or damaged, you can replace just that piece.

Resilient flooring. Vinyl, rubber, or linoleum flooring is relatively soft underfoot, yet firm, durable, and easy to clean. A textured surface guards against slipping.

Laundry, Crafts & Office Areas

Many homes today include certain rooms and areas set aside for specialized work—such as laundry rooms, craft areas, and home offices. Most such places are not usually designed for children, but children may spend time there if that's where they can be near mom or dad.

Put a lock on the door to these work areas or use doorknob sleeves (see page 35) so your baby can't go visiting without you. For times when your child keeps you company, here are other ways to make these places safer.

Laundry room

Both its big, warm, and noisy appliances and its colorful detergent boxes attract small children to the laundry room.

Childproof the room. Detergents, starches, bleaches, cleansers, fabric softeners, and stain removers can all be toxic and must be locked away or put in out-of-reach cabinets. Never store house-cleaning or laundry chemicals in containers designed for different products and don't leave any of these supplies sitting out on the washer or dryer. Be sure to wipe up any residue after use and dispose of empty containers in the outdoor trash.

For maximum safety, unplug the washer and dryer when not in use, always keep the washer lid and dryer door closed, and

Large plastic ring links together wire baskets holding laundry supplies so that little explorers can't get into them.

store mops, brooms, and other cleaning equipment in closed, safety-latched closets.

Iron with care. Wait until your child is napping, happy in a playpen, or otherwise unlikely to disturb you before ironing. All it takes is one small bump on the ironing board to send the heavy, hot iron tumbling down. A sturdy, built-in ironing board with a childproof latch on its cabinet door, such as the one shown on the facing page, is safest.

Never leave the iron sitting on top of the ironing board or within a child's reach while the iron is hot or cooling, and never leave it plugged in. Always set the iron where a child cannot reach it or its cord. As an extra precaution, you can purchase an iron that shuts itself off, should you forget, but still make it a

habit to pull out the plug the minute you're through.

Sewing & craft rooms

Keep spools, thimbles, needles, pins, scissors, and other paraphernalia locked or latched in drawers or cabinets (see page 11). Instead of having to put everything away each time you stop working, it's much easier to set aside a sewing area that can be locked away behind folding doors. Or purchase a sewing machine that shuts away in its own cabinet. When it's not in use, unplug and cover the sewing machine.

Keep toxic or otherwise dangerous craft or hobby supplies well out of your child's reach—or locked up. Read labels and use only with good ventilation.

Home offices

These rooms present new challenges in childproofing: you must protect your work from your child as well as the reverse. If it's in reach, you just might find your baby chewing on the floppy disk containing all of this year's tax information. If your home office doesn't have a door that can be locked, consider folding doors that can close off a desk or use a classic rolltop desk so you can easily lock up your work when you leave (see photographs on facing page).

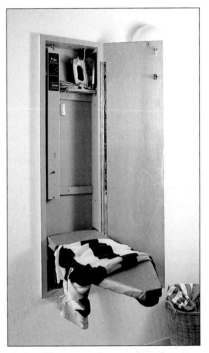

Now you see it, later you won't. *Built into a closet, this study shuts away behind folding doors when not in use. Watch out for little fingers when closing doors. Architect: David Jeremiah Hurley.*

Hot and heavy, *an iron can be a danger to tots who get too close. Here's a safe answer: shut it away in a cupboard when not needed. Design: Lizette Wilbur.*

Provide a cupboard nearby to fill with delights for baby: this will serve as a diversion while you work—at least for a short while.

Pencils, pens, erasers, paper clips, staples, rubber bands, typewriter ribbon—anything that is sharp or toxic or small enough to go into baby's mouth should be kept well away from small visitors to your office. Make sure that your telephone and its dangling cord stay out of baby's reach. Route electrical cords where your child can't get to them. Eliminate, hide, or tape down extension cords, and keep them unplugged and stored away when not in use. Cap or cover electrical outlets (see page 10).

When shut, *this rolltop desk protects mom's and dad's paperwork and privacy. Architect: Robert C. Peterson.*

Family Spaces

In the living areas of the house where the family relaxes, most furnishings are as inviting and safe for small children as for their elders. What could be safer than to sit in mommy's or daddy's lap in the comfort of a big, overstuffed chair?

But beyond the cushioned chair, many living rooms do contain places where a young child could get hurt—as well as pieces that a child could hurt. These details call for a parent's protective attention.

Child-friendly furniture

If chairs and couches are well padded with rugged upholstery and if tables have smooth, rounded edges and corners, your child and your furnishings can coexist happily with minimal risk.

Choose easy-care upholstery fabrics in patterns and colors least likely to advertise stains and wear-and-tear. Look into stain-repellent fabric finishes, whether applied by the manufacturer or sprayed on by you.

Tables and chairs. Tables with sharp, hard edges (especially marble or glass) injure many stumbling toddlers. Attach edge protectors and add corner guards (see page 14). Better yet is a table with smooth, rounded edges or one made of soft wicker (without protruding reed ends) or plastic.

Choose sturdy furniture. Make sure that all tabletops are anchored securely to their bases. A draping tablecloth is an invitation to an accident: a small child can grab the cloth for support (or simply out of curiosity) and pull down everything on the tabletop.

Tuck dining chairs under the table so your child won't be tempted to use them to climb up onto the tabletop.

Bookshelves. Check freestanding bookshelves for stability. If at all unsteady, they can be anchored with screws to wall studs. If that's not possible, use spreading anchors as shown on the facing page. Bookshelves with cabinet doors at the bottom are harder for kids to climb. And such cabinets provide a good place to keep small paraphernalia out of sight.

Wedging books tightly on shelves helps to foil the toddler's

Choose casual, soft, yet sturdy furniture for two reasons. It will be friendlier and often safer for young climbers, and it will survive the rigors of childhood in better condition.

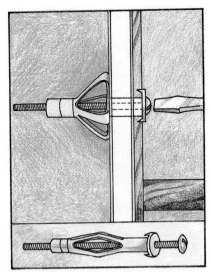

To secure freestanding bookshelves and cabinets to the wall, use spreading anchors.

game of pulling them all off the shelves. Breakables should go out of reach or behind locked doors. Be sure that china cabinets are stable, unclimbable, and have locks or safety latches on their doors.

Electronic equipment. For the safety of both your child and your expensive equipment, place your television, stereo, and other gear out of reach in cabinets, or at least against a wall (but with allowances for air circulation on all sides and on top to prevent overheating). If you keep the television behind closed doors now, it will be easier to monitor your child's viewing a little later on.

Lamps. All freestanding lamps, especially floor lamps, are easily pulled over. For ideal lamp safety, temporarily eliminate table and floor lamps in favor of wall- and ceiling-mounted lighting. If that's not possible, make sure that your lamps are sturdy and are placed where their cords drop out of sight and reach. If necessary, use 2-inch-wide clear packing tape to secure cords along the floor or baseboards. Reduce the wattage of lamps that have hot, bare bulbs beneath shades under which small fingers could reach. Never leave a lighting fixture without a bulb in its socket.

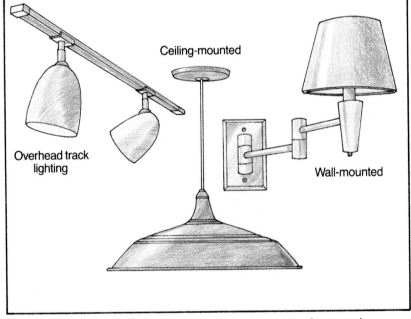

Light fixtures placed high on walls or on the ceiling offer more safety around inquisitive toddlers than floor or table lamps, which are easily knocked over.

Fireplaces, stoves & heaters

To guard against burns, buy a sturdy, rigid spark screen (not a mesh curtain) for the fireplace. Or have a fireplace shop install glass fireplace doors (but be aware that a child can open most types).

Wood stoves can be a problem because most get very hot; some are manufactured with a protective steel jacket that can reduce the possibility of burns. Or you can have a detachable screen custom-built—a costly solution. If you don't have a secure way to keep small children away from a wood stove, the best policy is not to fire it up until they're a little older and more self-protective.

Fire safety rules for using fireplaces and wood stoves are listed below (also see pages 72–75).

■ Never leave your child unattended when there is a fire in the fireplace or stove.

■ Keep fireplace tongs and other tools out of reach.

■ Don't close the damper until the fire is completely out.

■ Be sure there is sufficient ventilation (fresh air) when burning a fire.

■ Burn only firewood. Other materials could prove dangerous.

■ Have the flue inspected and cleaned once a year to prevent chimney fires.

Avoid burns from heaters by screening off radiators and heating registers that get hot. Use fireplace screens, bolting them in place if possible. *Note that floor furnaces, found in some older homes, are extremely dangerous,* with temperatures known to reach 300°F. Unless you have an effective method of blocking off a floor furnace, don't use it while children are in the house.

Other safety checkpoints

If you have houseplants, read through the feature on potentially harmful plants (see pages 46–47), which lists many, but not all, poisonous plants.

To be safest—and to minimize potential mess—suspend or set all houseplants well out of a toddler's reach.

Also read about durable and easily cleaned surfaces for walls and floor (see page 25). Remove scatter rugs or area rugs that might trip children. Tiny objects can get lost in deep-pile or shag carpeting. Have carpets professionally steam-cleaned, and vacuum often.

Eliminate extension cords and cover electrical receptacles (see page 10).

Low, soft furnishings covered with rugged fabrics make this home entertainment center practical for family members of every age. A safety-glass door seals off stereo in background. Design: Minimal Space.

Whether blazing in winter or cold in summer, this fireplace stays out of children's reach behind two sets of doors, one made of glass, the other made of fine mesh screening.

PROTECTING PARENTS' VALUABLES

Childproofing has two purposes: the first and most urgent is to protect your child from household hazards; the second is to protect your house and its contents from your child. Though this book focuses on protecting the child, preserving your house and valuables is also important. Here are a few techniques.

What you prize, move to where small children can't reach (after all, why shouldn't that crystal bird fly?). You may want to leave a few safe and replaceable items within reach to teach the meaning of "touch with only one fin-

Why hide your hobby in a drawer when you can display it on the wall? Mounted under glass, this framed collection of coins and currency is well protected.

How fascinating to a 2-year-old: knobs, lights, cassettes, and thunderous sound. To stop your child from experimenting, keep the stereo behind safety-latched doors. Architect: Vito Cetta & Associates.

ger." Don't forget the obvious: no one would want to find their 3-year-old with kiddy scissors, carefully snipping $20 bills into shreds.

Out of sight, out of mind: move visually tempting objects from view. Stow them behind closed doors, where they won't lure your child to climb the shelves. A typewriter, clarinet, set of golf clubs, or pair of satin shoes look irresistible to a young, imaginative child. It's easiest if they stay hidden except for rare occasions. If they have to stay in view, at least store them in sturdy cases or well out of a child's reach.

Store valuables and delicate items—cameras, table linens, and jewelry, for example—in drawers or cabinets with childproof latches (see page 11).

But there's no need to shut everything out of sight. You might want to hang favorite china plates high on the kitchen or dining room wall. Let children peep at delicate collectibles in a glass-front display cabinet. Make use of such out-of-reach locations as the fireplace mantel, piano top, or upper bookcase shelves.

Having collected them since she was a child herself, this mom isn't about to put away her prized plates. Instead, they decorate the kitchen walls, where they're easily seen and enjoyed but well out of a small daughter's reach.

31

Stairs & Walkways

Halls, stairs, and landings are a home's traffic routes—usually designed for adults to navigate, but not for children. Even so, kids love to race down hallways, play halfway up the stairs, and build nests on landings.

A flat, floor-level entry and hallway are relatively safe for children; you'll need to take only a few precautions to childproof them. Stairways and landings can involve greater risks of injury.

Lighting. Be sure all foot-traffic areas are well lighted without glare or shadows. Three-way light switches (to turn lights off or on from either end of the hall or stairs) are helpful. If your house isn't wired for these, plug

At the top of the stairs, a safety gate stops these little ones from exploring downward. Rigid panels of acrylic clamped at top and bottom to balusters prevent any chance of getting stuck or falling between them.

a night-light into a nearby outlet (include an outlet cover, as shown on page 10).

Sure footing. For clear, easy passage, remove toys and obstacles, eliminate loose rugs, and install nonslippery surfaces underfoot. Clean up spills immediately and keep your child from walking on wet floors.

Climbing skill. To a toddler, climbing stairs is an exciting accomplishment, as well as an exercise that develops coordination and muscles. Small children need to learn how to go up and down stairs properly (crawling down backwards is safest for toddlers). Accompany them while they're learning.

Safety gates and doors. At both the top and bottom of open stairs, install safety gates like the one shown on the facing page. Certain accordion-style gates have caused serious accidents (see pages 62–63 for more information on gates). Mount the gate securely with screws. A pressure-mounted type may not be reliable unless you can install it so tightly that your child can't budge it.

If there is a basement door or other door that your child shouldn't open at one end of the stairs, keep it closed and place a sleeve on the doorknob (see page 35).

Treads and risers. Make sure that stairs are in good structural condition and have slip-resistant tread surfaces. Wall-to-wall, low-pile carpeting is soft underfoot for both stairs and hallways, and gives some cushioning in case of a fall.

Stairs with open risers are dangerous for young kids, who can crawl right through them. Be especially watchful if your home has such a staircase; block it at top and bottom with fixed safety gates. Also be vigilant if you have a spiral staircase, because its turns can be difficult to negotiate; metal spiral staircases can have hard, sharp edges.

Keep stairs free of clutter. You'll invite stumbling if you use them for collecting items that need to go to the upper or lower floor.

Railings. An ideally child-safe stairway would have two parallel handrails on each side: one placed at a comfortable level for adults (30 to 34 inches above the tread's nosing) and a lower one placed where it can be easily grasped by children. You can buy railings and brackets at a building supply store. Screw the railing securely into wall studs.

Open railings of sturdy and smooth balusters can also give children a good grip as they climb stairs. These open railings on stairs, landings, and upper levels should be at least 36 inches high. If balusters are spaced widely enough that a small body could squirm between them, provide a barrier by temporarily clamping sheets of $\frac{1}{16}$-inch clear acrylic or styrene plastic to the railing or balusters using electronic cable ties.

Coach your crawling baby how to navigate stairs safely: when going down, your child should go backwards.

Windows & Doors

What's beyond that door? Can I crawl through this window to get outside? Thoughts like these must cross the minds of most small children as curiosity prompts them to new explorations. And that's why checking windows and doors is a very important part of making your home child-safe.

Consider fire safety

Always keep fire safety in mind when babyproofing windows and doors. Every room should have two escape routes: the main door and a secondary door or window. You'll want to protect your baby from crawling out a window or from opening an unsafe door, but adults and children older than toddler age must be able to open escape windows and doors quickly and easily.

Keep all escape routes clear and, for bedrooms on upper stories, provide escape ladders. Teach your children what to do in an emergency as soon as they are old enough to understand. (For more information on planning for fire safety, see page 72.)

Childproofing windows

The first step in safeguarding windows is to remove objects under windows that a child might climb. For example, rearrange chairs and tables to keep them at a distance from windows.

Of course, if a child has the will to get up to a window,

there's probably a way that he or she will eventually do it. So, you'll have to find a way to limit the window's opening size or create a barrier against falling out.

Don't rely on window screens as a barrier to keep kids in—a child can lean against a screen and tumble right through. You can block the openings with standard window grilles. Again, just be sure an adult or older child can release barrier from the inside in an emergency.

Several different kinds of locks are available for both windows and doors (see below).

A double-hung window can be locked shut with an ordinary sash lock or—for more security—

with keyed sash locks. If you choose keyed locks, hang the key on a screw next to the window, well above a small child's reach, where family members and babysitters can find it in an emergency.

For a window not needed as a fire escape, you can cut a thin block of scrap wood and nail it inside the upper track as a stop for the lower window section. Another method for this type of window is to screw the lower section to the frame and use the upper section for ventilation.

Sliding windows and doors can be protected in several ways. You can buy a keyed lock that fastens onto the slider's track or a shaped metal strip that clips onto the

A Charley bar, when down (in the horizontal position), stops a sliding window from opening. When raised to the vertical position and clipped in place, the sliding window can move.

A shaped metal clip, inserted into the lower track of a sliding window or door, keeps it fully or partially closed.

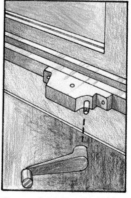

Removing the crank of a casement window makes it nearly impossible to operate the window. Store the crank nearby but out of a small child's reach.

track (see facing page). Bolt-action slider locks allow a door to be opened for ventilation. Again, if you use a keyed lock, hang the key nearby, in sight, in case of an emergency.

A "Charley bar" is easy to mount and, when in its "down" position, wedges a slider shut (see facing page). It can be raised and clipped to the wall or frame when you want to use the window or door.

A casement window—or any window with a crank—is easy to childproof just by removing the crank (see facing page); store the crank nearby. Or you can install a door-type safety chain.

Window coverings. Cut off or adjust shade, blind, or curtain cords to their shortest possible lengths and eliminate loops (window cords can strangle infants). If the window covering requires a long cord, screw a cleat or tie-down fixture to the wall (near the top of the window, if possible) and wrap or tie the cord around it.

Safety glass. Windows and doors that reach within 18 inches of the floor should be glazed with safety glass. Because even dealers and contractors are not always fully familiar with safety glass particulars, let your local building inspector guide you. To keep kids and adults from walking through —or slamming into—tall windows and sliding glass doors, stick a few colorful decals on them near eye level or place furniture in front of them.

Childproofing doors

When using doors, be careful, because children often "shadow" their parents around the house. It's easy for them to get caught in a slamming door or for their little fingers to get pinched in closing doors, particularly bi-fold doors or those with multiple sets of hinges.

Doorknob sleeves. To keep children from turning round door knobs, fit knobs with special plastic sleeves (see below).

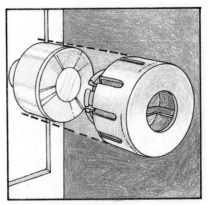

Only an adult's grip can manipulate the doorknob underneath this loose plastic sleeve.

To keep a door locked, install a safety chain, barrel bolt, pivot lock, or hook-and-eye that can't be reached by small kids (put it within reach of older children).

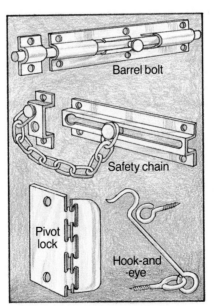

Barrel bolt

Safety chain

Pivot lock

Hook-and-eye

Simple locks such as those shown above can keep small children out of unsafe areas. But always place locks within reach of older kids in case of emergency.

To close a door automatically (important for doors that lead to particularly dangerous areas), you can mount a pneumatic or hydraulic automatic door-closer to the top of a door to ensure easy, gentle closing. Or, you can replace one or more of the hinges with spring-loaded, self-closing ones. Mount one, then test the door. If necessary, add another—but be sure the door doesn't slam shut (this can be dangerous and noisy).

Replace any solid door stops that might bounce a quickly opened door with flexible door stops mounted high on the door. If your home has any swinging doors, such as between the dining room and kitchen, consider replacing them with a standard or pocket door.

Safety gates. Several kinds of gates are available from baby supply stores for blocking doorways. Every home with a small child needs at least one or two. For a full discussion of this safety device, turn to pages 62–63.

Sounding an alarm

To alert you that an important door or window has been opened (a door that goes to the pool, for example), you can hang a small bell (with a loud gong) on the door or, better still, buy an electronic alarm that sounds when the door is opened or closed. Beware of too loud an alarm that could hurt your child's hearing (besides causing a scare). Several types are available:

■ A doorknob alarm that activates when the doorknob is touched

■ A magnetic-contact alarm that sounds a pleasant bong when the door it's protecting is opened

■ A plunger alarm that fits at the base of a sliding door's track and sounds when the door is opened

Playing It Safe Outdoors

Child safety in the backyard

Most kids love the outdoors. Like plants and trees, they thrive on sun and fresh air. Outdoors, they can delight in the sights, sounds, smells, and sensations of nature. Being out in the real world is important to them. (And, if you've ever been housebound with a toddler for more than a day or so, you know that parents need to get out, too!)

So that your child can play safely outdoors, you'll want to make your yard and outdoor play areas as free as possible of hazards. And you'll need to help your child learn to recognize and avoid dangerous objects, activities, and situations.

Even if your baby's outdoor experiences are limited now to sheltered rides in the stroller or to wriggles on a lawn blanket, you might as well get a head start on childproofing. Before you know it, baby will become an inquisitive toddler, testing and tasting everything within reach.

Here are some of the ways this chapter can help you childproof your garden and play area: it will show you how to make your deck or porch into a safe outdoor play room; how to safeguard the garage, workshop, or other work center; how to plan and create a fun, safe play yard and choose safe outdoor play equipment; how to protect your child from the swimming pool and other bodies of water; and how to put up a reliable fence. You'll even find a special feature on unsafe plants.

Decks & Porches

Most ground-level decks and porches are great places for kids to cut loose and enjoy high-energy play. Decks and porches are usually comfortable, flat, open spaces that are rugged enough to hold up to plenty of roughhousing.

But any deck, porch, or balcony above the first floor can't be considered safe for unsupervised child's play—no matter how secure you make its railings.

Making a safety check

Here's what to check and, as necessary, to improve to make your ground-floor deck or porch a safe, friendly play environment for children.

Railings prevent falls. Make sure that your railings circle the entire porch or deck play area, providing a sturdy barrier that children can't squeeze through, climb over, slide under, or get caught in.

A porch or deck railing should be at least 36 inches high with no more than 2⅜ inches between vertical members.

One way to close gaps between rails is to cut and staple 2½- by 2-inch (or finer) vinyl-coated wire mesh to the railing, as shown on the facing page. Make sure that all staples are firmly secured. With wire cutters, trim off any cut ends. (For more on this kind of fencing, see page 53.)

For a more elegant—but more expensive—solution, you can attach clear panels of acrylic or styrene plastic (see page 32). These materials are sold by building and home improvement retail stores, which will sometimes cut them to size for you.

Check the floor of your deck or porch. Though it will mean hard work, it will also mean a much safer play area if you strip away any old chipped or peeling paint, which may be toxic.

Also beware of preservative-treated wood, which could put a child in direct contact with toxic chemicals. Some can be painted over, but some don't take painting. Check with your lumber supplier for advice. Dispose of any scrap or sawdust from treated lumber in the trash or bury it, but do not burn it.

Patch holes, repair loose boards, pound home loose or protruding nails, and sand away slivers. Check that floors are not unduly slippery when wet. Non-slip fiberglass surfacing or outdoor carpeting are great surfaces for decks and porches.

Gently swaying porch swing, its ropes securely anchored to the ceiling, gives this tot a taste of the outside world without having to go far from home.

*A **wide safety gate** fences off a cul-de-sac at one end of this porch, creating a protected play area for those too young to roam freely in the backyard.*

***Securely fenced** with wire mesh, a sunny deck makes a comfortable play surface for adult-supervised preschoolers. Design: Scott Fitzgerrell.*

Block stairs from small adventurers. It's simplest to use a safety gate securely fastened to sturdy posts, not simply pressure-mounted. If the entry opening is too wide, fence off part of the porch or deck area to keep your child away from the stairs, as shown above.

Pick up any small or otherwise unsafe objects that your child could reach and put into his or her mouth, ear, or nose. Move potted plants.

Safeguard electrical receptacles in the deck or porch area by replacing them with ground fault circuit interrupters (see page 19). Also block them with bulky furniture or locking outdoor receptacle covers. Block off or remove light fixtures that a child could reach. Keep electrical cords out of reach. Make sure that no insecticides or electrical bug-killing devices remain in the area.

Equipment & furniture

For a safer deck or porch, use patio furniture that won't pinch fingers, tip easily, or fold up suddenly. Make sure that edges are reasonably smooth and rounded, not sharp or splintered. Be sure that painted furniture and deck components are nontoxic.

Choose a ceiling-mounted porch swing, rather than a free-standing one that could pinch fingers or arms against its stand. Consider laying down a tumbling mat for gymnastics and horseplay.

Place furniture so that your child can't use it to climb up and over the deck or porch railing.

Decks and porches are favorite sites for family barbecues (but if small or cramped, not the safest sites). While your child is small, it's best to move the barbecue grill elsewhere, or provide a barrier. And keep starter fluid, propane, briquettes, barbecue tools, and other supplies well out of children's reach or locked safely away.

Garage & Work Areas

Fascinating tools and machinery make garages, garden sheds, storage areas, and workshops dangerously appealing to children. But unless you're working there on a special project with your child, keep these areas strictly off limits. Most garages and workshops are catchalls for so many sharp tools and machines, as well as poisons and fuels, that it is impossible to make them really safe.

Your strategy in these areas should be to block entry but also to try to minimize risk if your child gets in anyway.

Locking & opening the door

With small children poking around at home, it's well worth the slight hassle of keeping doors to the garage, workshop, garden shed, and similar areas securely locked. Hasps and locking garage doors can do the job (see page 35 for other possibilities).

If your garage has an automatic garage door, be sure that its operating switch is placed well out of your child's reach. Many kids discover the thrilling—and perilous—game of racing under the door before it closes. As a partial safeguard, however, be sure the door operator has a pressure-sensitive device that will cause the door to stop or reverse direction when an object is encountered. But even this technology offers no ironclad guarantee against at least minor injury to playful kids.

If the garage has a roll-up garage door, be sure the channels between each panel have a rubber cushioning strip or are shaped to prevent finger pinching. For safety's sake, teach kids that the garage door is dangerous.

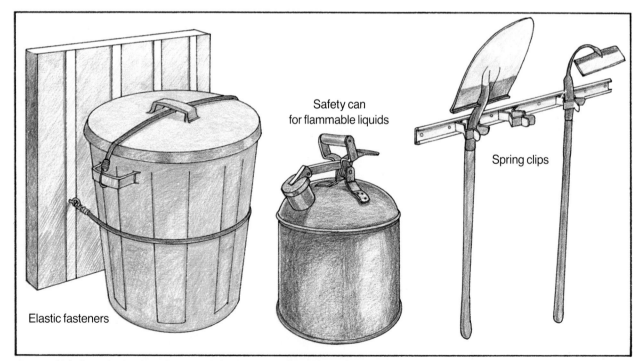

Safety can for flammable liquids

Spring clips

Elastic fasteners

To stop kids from tipping it over, secure garbage can to wall (and lid to can) with heavy elastic cords (left). Store dangerous flammable liquids in a UL-marked safety can (center) in a well-ventilated area far from heat sources, never in the house. With handles resting on the ground, spring-clip garden tools upright (right).

Lockable doors keep children from getting into materials that could harm them. They also hide garbage cans and supplies from view. Architect: The Hastings Group.

Organizing for safety

No matter how conscientious you are about locking doors, there could easily come a day when you forget and your child manages to get into the work area. So, store harmful objects as inaccessibly as you can.

Keep work areas as clutter-free as possible. Put away tools after use. *Always unplug power tools after use.*

Dispose of unneeded chemicals (following label directions) and lock up those you do need—well out of your child's reach.

To stop pint-sized intruders, put child-safe latches, shown on page 11, on cabinets. To stop older kids (or young ones who can get past the latches), you'll need real locks on cabinets storing dangerous materials.

For the whole family's fire safety, *store flammable liquids in a safety can* with a spring closure (shown on facing page). Use a can with a UL or FM (Underwriters Laboratory or Factory Mutual) mark. Rags that have soaked up flammables should be disposed of in the outdoor trash can after hanging them outdoors to dry.

Other safeguards

As described on page 73, install a smoke detector in the work area. Keep an A-B-C fire extinguisher near the garage or work-shop exit.

An unsuspected hazard sometimes stored in garages is an *unused refrigerator.* Kids can climb into these, close the door, become trapped, and, if not quickly discovered, can suffocate. Lock or block off the door, or remove it entirely.

Fishing tackle, like most of what we store in the garage, should be kept safely out of children's reach. Heavy, lockable doors like these are a good precaution. Design: Jean Chappell.

41

Backyard & Play Area

Whether squeezing behind a tree for hide-and-seek, studying ladybugs on dandelions, or learning to catch a slow pitch, most children delight in outdoor play. Though your yard may seem like a safe place for kids, the chances are good that it isn't a perfectly benign play zone. (A list of harmful plants on pages 46–47 will help you know whether what you're growing is safe, although not every species is included.)

Sprucing up

Children have an amazing ability to ferret out anything that's not good for them—or that's dangerous. In your garden, if there's glass to be stepped on by a bare foot, a beehive to unsettle, or a hole to fall into, kids are likely to oblige. One of a parent's jobs is to eliminate such potential accidents—as often as possible. Keeping a child-safe yard makes the job much easier. Start by sprucing up the area.

Comb the ground, little by little, for anything that might cause trouble: bottles, soft-drink cans, broken glass, tools, sharp sticks, rocks, cigarette butts, boards with nails, protruding pipes, wires, ropes, old auto parts, old containers of fertilizer or insecticide, barbecue equipment, or lighter fluid. Your yard may not conceal any of these troublemakers. But then again, you just might find a few hidden under bushes or in an overgrown corner.

Fill in and cover any ponds or abandoned wells. Also fill in any holes, including places that become puddles after rainfall (small children can drown in just a few inches of water). Remove any standing water and fill in the basins that held it.

Store yard equipment where your child can't get to it. Put a hasp and lock on storage sheds that children might get into. Keep garbage cans inaccessible behind a fence, in a shed, or attached as shown on page 40.

Stack firewood, lumber, and building materials away from play areas. Such piles are tempting to climb, but can topple easily; they can also attract rodents and snakes.

Securely fence off any dangerous areas of the yard, such as a steep drop-off or thorny growth. It's especially important to fence off pools and spas (see page 50).

Friendly ground covers

Are the ground surfaces around your house hard or soft? Are they forgiving of falls, friendly for children's games and active play? Or could some of the surfaces hurt a small child?

Wood play structure has soft swing seats suspended over a carpet of redwood bark to cushion any falls. Grass, bordered by a concrete bike path, offers another inviting play surface. Landscape architect: Taro Yamagami.

A concrete slab or asphalt area is a great surface for wheeled toys. But underneath play equipment, it makes for a hard landing.

Wood chips, bark, or sand can help absorb the impact of a child's fall—in most cases—without resulting in injury. Under play equipment, spread a 6-inch layer of sand or 5 to 6 inches of bark or wood chips. (Coarsely ground fir bark causes fewer splinters than pine bark.) Wet it down to keep it from blowing in windy weather. However, wet sand can become quite hard. Sawdust is not safe, since it may harbor splinters or even nails and can be allergenic.

Since most of these ground covers can be scooped up into baby's mouth, be vigilant. Though a little swallowed sand hasn't hurt most of us, children can get worms if cats use the sand as a litter box.

Grass lawns create broad, relatively soft expanses, inviting for all kinds of children's games. Most seed companies sell rugged grass mixtures; choose one without clover, which attracts bees. However, grass may be slightly less cushioning than other ground covers.

Safer yard work

Leaves, flowers, grass, dirt, songbirds, and breezes are joyful discoveries to children. But nobody wants a child to discover a pair of pruning shears on the garden path—or to take an interest in the lawn mower.

When working outside with hand tools, be especially careful not to leave them within a child's reach; most garden tools can be quite dangerous.

Never use the power lawn mower, whether it's a walk-behind or riding type, if a child is nearby. Rocks and other sharp debris hurled by whirling mower blades have caused serious injury to children. After mowing the lawn, a power mower—or any other machine with a gas engine —will stay hot for a while. Shut it away immediately in ventilated storage behind locked doors.

Make it a habit to keep garden gates latched. For gates to a busy street, a pool, or gardening supplies, it's safest to use self-closing and self-latching hardware (see page 52).

With little ones exploring the garden, you may have to change some of your garden-care products to those that are least toxic. Use fertilizers that dissolve in water and spread immediately into the soil; pellets and other residue can too easily be tasted.

Play structures

Most kids can spin creative play from rocks or pinecones or anything they find outdoors. But nothing quite stimulates a young child like a well-designed outdoor play structure. Swings, slides, and climbers are a child's dream come true.

In recent years, outdoor play structures have undergone a design revolution. Old pipe-frame swingsets have taken a back seat to complex outdoor edifices of timber, tires, and heavy rope. Intended to inspire children's imaginations, most of these new playground creations have also been built for safety. Even so, inspect them yourself for secure fastenings, sure footing, solidity of rope and net, smooth and unsplintered wood,

For safety, comfort, and delight, nothing beats a fat inner tube swing.

...backyard & play areas

and absence of openings that could entrap a child's body or head.

When building a play yard, you'll need to know the safety basics of outdoor play equipment. Because of toxicity, do not use treated wood unless there will be only occasional skin contact. Instead, use naturally weather-resistant redwood or cedar. Here are some further considerations.

Cushioning falls. Taking a fall is one of the common mishaps when children play on swings, slides, or climbers. It helps if play equipment is located over a soft, cushioned surface, such as a thick layer of wood chips, bark, sand, grass (see pages 42–43), or rubber matting. Play equipment should not be set up over hard concrete or asphalt.

Locating equipment. At home, place play equipment at least 6 feet from house walls, fences, trees, or other obstacles, especially if the equipment includes swings.

Make sure the equipment is level and anchor it firmly in the ground. Set each post for a swingset in a concrete hole at least 9 inches square. Also make sure that the swingset has been correctly assembled. Tighten all nuts and bolts. Cut off protruding bolt ends with a hacksaw.

Safe swings. Prevent injuries in case the swing seat hits a child by making sure that it's made of a soft material, such as rubber or rubberized canvas.

For small children up to about age 2½ or 3, provide full-support bucket seats that they won't tumble out of. For older kids, a big inner tube makes a safe, inexpensive swing.

Attach a swing to wood only with a heavy bolt or eye bolt that penetrates all the way through and is secured by a locknut. A screw eye will loosen with the swing's motion and eventually come loose. Also, check all wood play equipment occasionally because it's subject to rot.

For swings, smooth, strong plastic ropes are gentler for young children than chains. Take the ropes down during a rainy or snowy winter. Replace S-hooks (which might disconnect one day) with connector hooks equipped with spring closures or locking O-rings.

The sandbox. A favorite of very young children, the sandbox is usually the safest piece of play equipment. Keep it covered when not in use so cats stay away from it. Make sure its frame is free of loose nails and splinters. Fill it with coarse washed ocean sand (or river sand).

Safe sliding. A slide for small children should be wide, not too high, and not too steep (see photo on facing page). All slides should have steps that are easy for a tot to climb and a solid railing to grip. The sliding surface should have sides at least 2½ inches high. Slides built into the side of a hill are safer, because there's less chance of injury; also safer are slides enclosed by a chute.

Be cautious with a metal slide on a hot, sunny day; it could absorb enough heat to burn. At home, place the slide in the shade if you can. If you're building a slide yourself, face it with cool plastic laminate in a light color, which will reflect heat. Apply a nonslip coating on steps (or on ladder rungs of a purchased slide).

Easily climbable, this structure provides hours of play for small kids who would be less safe on bigger, metal climbing bars. *Design: Sam and Rita Eisenstat.*

A tire swing makes a relatively soft impact if collision occurs—one of the commonest accidents on playgrounds. *Design: Peter O. Whiteley.*

Climbing structures. Make sure that all components are sturdy and securely fastened together. Check for areas between railings or surfaces that might entrap a small head or body part, or snag clothing. You'll want your children to clamber over these structures without danger of harm if they should fall, so spread a soft surface beneath, as mentioned earlier.

Children should use climbing equipment only when it's dry; moisture makes it slippery. Make sure that a wood climber is free of splinters. Though toddlers are not likely to use them, don't allow play with rings that could entrap a child's head or limb.

Wading pools. Small children love to splash in these during hot weather. The soft, inflatable kind of pool is safest, as well as inexpensive. Be sure to stay near your child and not to leave even for a minute while he or she is in the pool. It takes only a few inches of water for a small child to drown.

For the first trip down, *a wide and not-too-steep slide is less intimidating, and safer, than larger types. Design: Peter O. Whiteley.*

Playing by the rules

Basic to play yard safety, whether at home, at a park, or at preschool, are a few rules. Even very young kids catch on quickly if taught simple rules in a friendly spirit.

■ Don't throw sand. This might not be the most consequential rule of childhood, but for many of us it's the first. Its corollary is not to throw or eat wood chips, toys, pebbles, or other play yard materials.

■ Use equipment safely and as it's meant to be used. In most cases, this means not to experiment too freely with the possibilities of a swing or slide. When a crowd of kids plays together, this rule has to be more stringent.

■ Watch out for others. Being hit by a swing is one of the biggest causes of playground injury; kids need to watch out where they walk. Falling from a climber or slide ladder is another danger. Teach kids to wait for their turns and not to push others.

Outdoor playthings

Anyone who has ever walked through a preschool yard during recess knows that young kids are not adverse to loud, active play. Small daredevils pilot kiddy cars and trikes through tot-sized demolition derbys; junior little-leaguers zip balls back and forth; budding contractors build cities and freeways, while pint-sized cooks stir up sandbox cuisine.

Such play often involves toys. Fortunately, today's children's products are often designed and tested to meet industry and sometimes government safety standards. These standards generally ensure that an item won't present a hazard— if it's used appropriately. Of course, children have a way of stretching a toy's use to brave new dimensions.

Before purchase, give all outdoor gear a careful inspection to be sure that it will hold up to years of hard use. Choose quality equipment suitable for your child's age and skill level. Stay away from breakable plastics. It's better to buy a few items of good, durable design than to buy many of cheaper construction. For more about safe toys, see page 64.

PLANTS TO AVOID

Tidbits from the plant kingdom —flowers, seeds, fruits, leaves, twigs, and bark—can look tempting to taste. But some can make a young body quite sick (usually only if ingested in quantity), and a few can even prove fatal. Teach your children early never to taste or pick plants growing indoors, in the garden, or in the wilds, without your permission.

Harmful plants generally have one of two effects. Toxic plants bring on illness, often gastroenteritis; some can even cause death. Injurious plants cause irritation—often intense—to the mouth, throat and tongue, or skin. If your youngster shows any of these symptoms and you suspect the cause is a plant, contact your pediatrician or poison control center immediately for advice. It will help if you have a cutting of the plant or know its name.

Listed on these two pages are common garden plants and house plants that are potentially toxic or injurious. It would be impossible to list every plant culprit, especially the many that grow in the wild. ***Be extremely careful of mushrooms, which do cause fatalities***. Be sure to identify whatever you're growing at home, indoors or out. Consult a good local nursery, as well as the *AMA Handbook of Poisonous and Injurious Plants*, published by the American Medical Association (available at public libraries).

Toxic plants

■ *Aconitum* (Monkshood, Wolfsbane). All parts are toxic.

■ *Adenium* (Desert Rose, Mock Azalea). All parts are toxic.

■ *Aesculus* (Horsechestnut, Buckeye). Nuts and twigs are toxic.

■ *Aloe.* Thick sap is toxic.

■ *Amaryllis* (Belladonna Lily, Naked Lady). Bulb is toxic.

■ *Avocado.* Leaves are toxic.

■ *Baptisia* (False Indigo, Wild Indigo). All parts are toxic.

■ *Brugmansia* (Jimson Weed, Mad Apple). All parts are toxic.

■ *Caesalpinia* (Poinciana). Seeds of most species are toxic.

■ *Caltha* (Marsh-marigold, Cowslip). All parts are toxic and irritating.

■ *Colchicum* (Autumn Crocus— not a true crocus). All parts are extremely toxic.

Convallaria majalis, *Lily-of-the-valley, looks too pretty to be deadly. Actually, it's quite dangerous. Don't let it grow in your garden.*

■ *Convallaria majalis* (Lily-of-the-valley). All parts are extremely toxic, as well as water plant was in.

■ *Corynocarpus* (New Zealand Laurel). Fruit is extremely toxic.

■ *Crinum.* All parts are toxic, including bulb.

■ *Daphne mezereum* (February Daphne). All parts are toxic.

■ *Digitalis purpurea* (Foxglove). Leaves are extremely toxic.

■ *Duranta* (Golden Dewdrop). Berries are toxic.

■ *Eriobotrya* (Loquat, Japanese Plum). Pit kernel inside fruit is toxic.

■ *Euonymus europaeus* (European Spindle Tree, Burning Bush). Fruit is toxic.

■ *Euphorbia* (Candelabra Cactus, Crown of Thorns, Poinsettia). Sap of some is toxic, also may cause skin irritation.

■ *Gelsemium* (Carolina Jessamine, Wood Vine). All parts are toxic.

■ *Gloriosa* (Glory Lily). All parts are toxic, especially tuberous root.

■ *Hedera* (English Ivy). Berry and leaf are toxic.

■ *Helleborus* (Christmas Rose). All parts are toxic.

■ *Hydrangea* (Hills-of-snow, Hortensia). Flower buds are toxic.

■ *Hymenocallis* (Peruvian Daffodil). Bulbs are toxic.

■ *Ilex* (Holly). Berries are toxic.

■ *Iris* (Fleur-de-lis). Roots are toxic.

■ *Kalmia* (Mountain Laurel). Leaves and nectar are toxic.

■ *Laburum* (Goldenchain Tree, Bean Tree). All parts are toxic, especially seeds.

■ *Lantana camara.* Immature berries are toxic.

■ *Leucothoe* (Dog Hobble). All parts of plant are toxic.

■ *Ligustrum* (Privet, Lovage). All parts are toxic.

■ *Lycoris* (Spider Lily, Hurricane Lily). Bulbs are toxic.

■ *Melia* (Chinaberry, Hog Bush). Fruit and bark are toxic.

■ *Myoporum.* Leaves and fruit are toxic.

■ *Narcissus* (Daffodil, Jonquil). Bulbs are toxic.

■ *Nerium* (Oleander). All parts are extremely toxic, including smoke from branches, water that plant was in, branches used as barbecue skewers.

■ *Ornithogalum* (Wonder Flower). All parts are toxic, especially bulb.

■ *Pachyrhizus* (Jicama). Root is edible but seeds and pods are toxic.

■ *Pernettya.* Leaves and nectar are toxic.

■ *Physalis* (Lantern Plant, Ground Cherry). Unripe berries are toxic.

■ *Pieris* (Fetterbush). Leaves and nectar are toxic.

■ *Potato.* Green tuber skin and uncooked shoots are toxic.

■ *Prunus* (Apricot, Cherry, Nectarine, Peach, Plum, Prune). Pit kernels are toxic.

■ *Rhamnus* (Black Dogwood, Coffeeberry). Bark and fruit are toxic.

■ *Rhododendron* (also Azalea). Leaves and honey from nectar are toxic.

■ *Rhubarb.* Stalks are wholesome but leaves are toxic.

■ *Ricinus* (Castor Bean). Plump seeds, usually white with black or brown mottling, are extremely toxic.

■ *Robinia pseudoacacia* (False Acacia). Bark, leaves, and seeds are toxic.

■ *Scilla* (Sea Onion, Bluebell). All parts are toxic.

■ *Sesbania* (Scarlet Wisteria Tree). All parts are toxic.

■ *Solanum* (Deadly Nightshade). Some species (all parts of plant) are fatal.

■ *Sophora* (Texas Mountain Laurel). Seeds are toxic.

Monstera deliciosa, *Split-leaf Philodendron, is a popular houseplant. But if tasted, its leaves burn the mouth area.*

■ *Symphoricarpos* (Snowberry). Berries are toxic if taken in quantity.

■ *Symphytum* (Comfrey). Leaves are toxic.

■ *Taxus* (Yew, Ground Hemlock). Most of plant, including seeds, is toxic.

■ *Thevetia peruviana* (Yellow Oleander). All parts are toxic, especially seeds.

■ *Wisteria.* All parts are toxic.

■ *Zephyranthes* (Rain Lily). Bulb is toxic.

Injurious plants

■ *Alocasia* (Elephant's Ear). Leaves and stems burn mouth area.

■ *Anthurium.* Leaves and stems burn mouth area.

■ *Arum* (Black Calla, Solomon's Lily). All parts hurt mouth and throat area.

■ *Buxus* (Boxwood). Irritates skin or, if eaten, causes nausea.

■ *Caladium.* All parts burn mouth area.

■ *Caryota* (Fishtail Palm). Fruit burns mouth area, irritates skin.

■ *Colocasia* (Elephant's Ear, Taro). Leaves burn mouth area.

■ *Dieffenbachia* (Dumb Cane). Leaves burn mouth area (have even caused temporary speech impairment), also irritate skin.

■ *Epipremnum* (Pothos). All parts irritate skin and, if eaten, cause diarrhea.

■ *Ficus benjamina.* Sap is injurious.

■ *Monstera* (Breadfruit Vine, Split-leaf Philodendron). Leaves burn mouth area.

■ *Philodendron.* Leaves burn mouth and throat area, also irritate skin.

■ *Pyracantha.* Berries and thorns are injurious.

■ *Spathiphyllum.* All parts burn mouth and throat area.

■ *Xanthosoma* (Blue Taro). Leaves burn mouth area.

■ *Zantedeschia* (Calla Lily). Leaves burn mouth and lips.

Swimming Pools & Spas

When summer rolls around, a swimming pool attracts people of all ages to its shimmering blue water. On a hot day, it may become the focus of family fun.

Unfortunately, children lack a healthy respect for the water's potential danger. Curiosity draws them near. In states where pools are numerous, there are even more fatalities to young children from drowning than from traffic accidents.

For this reason, it makes sense to teach children how to swim fairly soon. Do not rely on baby's swimming lessons, though. Throughout childhood, whether or not they can swim, *children should be watched at the pool by an adult capable of rescuing them*—one adult per each nonswimmer. Tell babysitters to keep children out of the pool enclosure.

Safeguarding the pool area

Kids, by nature, try to foil whatever barriers adults set up. For safety's sake around a pool, create several backups to ensure that neither your child nor neighborhood kids can gain access to your pool.

Among your choices are fences and gates (a building code requirement in many communities), a pool cover, and an alarm that gives a last-minute warning.

Pool covers. Designed to keep kids out, pool covers, such as the one shown on the facing page, are probably the surest barrier if designed and used correctly. A safe pool cover must be able to support an adult's weight.

To keep children out of the water reliably, the pool cover should attach securely in place. If rainwater collects, pump or drain the water away immediately; a few inches of water in a sagging pool cover could endanger a small child.

When people are swimming in the pool, remove the cover completely. Otherwise, there's the chance that someone could become trapped under it. And whenever adults are not at poolside, lock the cover in place.

Dad stands protectively by as she paddles in the pool's shallow end; her inflatable ring is not a reliable life preserver.

As a safety backup to a pool fence, install a sturdy pool cover. This one rolls out automatically. Cover should be strong enough to support an adult's weight. Remove it completely whenever anyone enters the pool.

High, fine mesh fencing provides a safe barricade around a swimming pool. Besides being unclimbable, this fence allows visibility, just in case a youngster gets into the pool area in spite of it.

...swimming pools & spas

Fences. A standard cover may not fit a pool that is very large or irregularly shaped. Even with a cover, a child-safe pool should be fenced to keep it securely off limits between supervised swims. Keep furniture and similar objects away from the fence, because they could be used for climbing.

A self-closing, self-latching gate assures that the gate won't be accidentally left open. A lockable gate provides extra security.

Pool fences are often regulated, sometimes stringently, by building codes. Usually, the fence must be 5 to 6 feet high, with slats or uprights spaced no wider than 4 inches. If a side of the house or other building serves as a portion of the pool area fence, it should have no doors or windows. Fencing must also stand far enough from the pool's edge to allow safe passage—at least 3 feet. Check with your local building department for other requirements.

Alarms. One type of pool alarm screeches when a heavy object, such as a person, falls into the water (the wave that results sets off the alarm). You would have to be relatively close in order for the alarm to provide a safe warning. And the alarm needs regular testing. Also, the sensitive mechanism may give you heart-wrenching false alarms.

Another type of alarm system for pools shoots a light beam around the water's perimeter (the same method is used at the entrance to some stores). The sound activates if the beam is broken. Again, you must be close enough to hear the alarm, but this kind gives you a warning before your child plunges into the water. False alarms can be a nuisance.

Pool equipment. Locate the pool heater, filter, and other equipment behind sturdy fencing or walls at least 5 feet high. Keep pool chemicals far from children's reach, preferably locked away.

Pool area upkeep. Have the pool deck repaired if damaged. If it's especially slippery, you can coat it with a nonslip surfacing material. Move away steps to an above-ground pool when the pool is not in use.

Use only unbreakable plates and glasses at poolside; allow no glass. Keep toys away from the area; a child can fall into the water while playing.

Protect all electrical outlets and equipment, as well as circuits for support equipment, with ground fault circuit interrupters

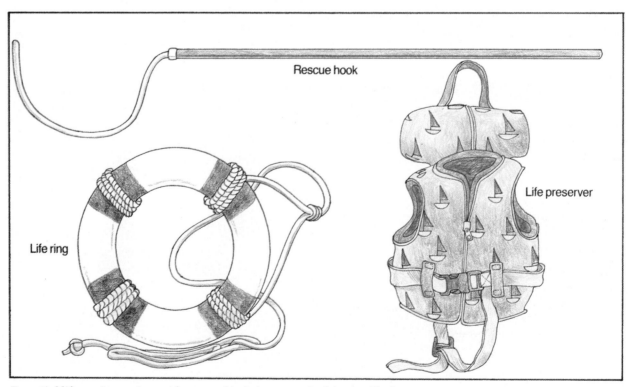

Rescue hook

Life preserver

Life ring

Essential life-saving equipment *for any pool includes a rescue hook (top), a life ring with a rope (left), and a USCG-approved life preserver, or personal flotation device, for a child (right); the preserver's pillow-like collar keeps the head above water.*

(see page 19). Test your GFCIs monthly. Inspect electrical equipment frequently and do not use the pool until any needed repairs are made. Do not allow electrical appliances inside the fenced pool area.

Keep a telephone near the pool so you don't have to go indoors to answer a call. Keep emergency numbers posted on the telephone.

Safe pool use

When small children are in the pool area, watch them continuously; never leave, even for a minute. Mark the pool's deep end with a rope supported by floats and don't allow nonswimmers or young beginning swimmers to go beyond the rope.

Another sound safety measure is to insist that young nonswimmers wear life preservers, also called personal flotation devices, or PFDs, while in the pool area. When buying a PFD, look for "USCG (U.S. Coast Guard) approved" on its label (one such life preserver is shown on the facing page). If there are several children or you're having a party, protect your toddler with a PFD even while you're standing nearby. Never leave a child alone in the pool enclosure and don't rely on a PFD or any inflatable device to prevent drowning. These measures are safety backups only.

Post pool rules (such as those above at right) near the pool. Keep a first-aid kit handy as well as life-saving equipment—a life ring with ³⁄₁₆-inch rope and a 10-foot rescue (shepherd's) hook. Learn lifesaving and cardio-pulmonary resuscitation (CPR) from a local hospital, American Red Cross chapter, or other community resource.

Make sure that the pool's water has been correctly treated

SUGGESTED POOL RULES

Listed below are a few rules that will help ensure the safety of young children in or near a swimming pool. But they also apply to anyone using a pool, no matter what their age or skill level.

■ *Nonswimmers* must be accompanied in the water by an adult who can swim. There must be one adult to each nonswimming child.

■ *Children may not enter the pool area* without an adult who can swim.

■ *No one may ever swim alone.*

■ *No running, pushing, or rough play* is allowed in or near the pool.

■ *No diving is allowed* unless the pool has an area designed for it.

■ *Glass and electrical appliances* are not allowed in the pool area; they can cause injury or electrocution.

■ *No one may swim if ill or injured;* bacteria can contaminate water.

■ *No swimming is allowed during a thunderstorm,* because the water attracts lightning.

■ *Night swimming is usually unsafe* for children unless closely supervised by adult swimmers in a well-lit pool. No one should swim at night in a dimly lit pool.

so that it's clean but not irritating from concentrated chlorine. Never use the pool when an automatic pool cleaner is operating, because its hoses can entangle a young swimmer.

Spa & hot tub safety

The hot, bubbly fun of a spa often delights children as much as their parents—and a family soak is a cozy experience.

But, besides the possibility of drowning, the water in a hot tub or spa poses another danger to young children. Even at a relatively moderate temperature comfortable for adults, water can scald young, sensitive skin. *For infants and young children, keep the water temperature no higher than 95°F and the soaking time no longer than 10 minutes.* Introduce

the child slowly to the hot water to be sure there's no discomfort or fear.

Never allow young children in the spa without an adult. Don't leave them, even for a minute. The strong circulating action of the pump can pull a child off balance (if this is the case, turn off the pump while soaking with your child). Beware of some older spas which have floor drains that create such strong suction that small children can be pulled underwater (see your dealer about replacing the drain). *Maintain the spa's cleanliness* as rigorously as you would the pool. The spa also needs the same protective fencing or sturdy locking cover.

Fences & Gates

Setting safe limits for children is a basic job for all parents. In the early years, you may have to set literal, physical boundaries for your child's protection. Though fences and gates can never be a substitute for a parent's attentiveness, they do offer a real measure of security and peace of mind.

Choosing the right fence

Several styles of fencing will keep children in a play yard or away from a busy street or swimming pool.

For a toddler or small child, a fence that's 4 to 4½ feet high is enough. Choose unclimbable fencing, with no toeholds in posts, frame, rails, or mesh.

Besides being high enough and unclimbable, a protective fence for young children should allow adequate visibility. If the fencing is wire mesh, you can keep an eye on the little ones as they play; solid boards would not allow that. Visibility is even more important when fencing a pool area.

Keep outdoor furniture, garbage cans, and anything a child might use as a ladder away from the fence. Check along the fence occasionally. Sometimes a dog will burrow under a fence, leaving a depression big enough for a child to crawl through. Clear away any protruding nails, wire ends, or splinters.

The gate

A child-safe gate should swing freely and close securely. To accommodate people who forget to close the gate, attach self-closing hinges or a gate spring. Also install self-latching gate hardware. Most of these come with a padlock eye for added security when the gate gives access to a dangerous area, such as a garden work center or swimming pool.

A selection of self-latching gate hardware is shown at left.

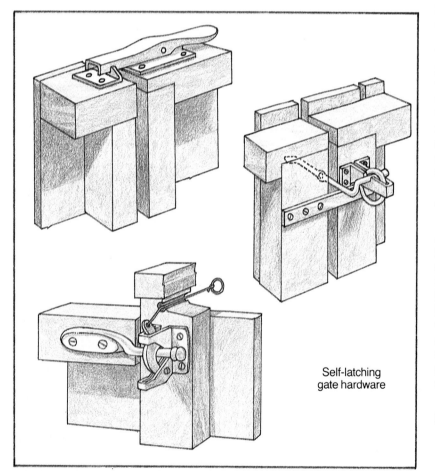

Self-latching
gate hardware

Choose from a variety of self-latching hardware for outdoor gates. Used with a gate spring, the gate will close and latch itself, keeping small children safe inside the play yard fence.

FENCING THEM IN

Do you need to keep adventurous toddlers within bounds? Here's an easy way to do so. Build a temporary fence of welded wire mesh and steel posts to turn your front yard or backyard into a safe play area. The fence goes up fast and easily, yet with sturdy results. Its mesh lets you see your children at play. The whole project is relatively low in cost, and the fence is easy to disassemble when the kids no longer need it.

Basic materials. You'll need welded, vinyl-coated wire mesh fencing in which a child can't get a toehold. For a safe play yard, choose 4-foot-wide fencing with 5-foot companion steel posts.

Planning a fence. Plan for enough fencing to stretch the length of each run or each straight side of the play area. You'll also need one post for the end of each run, plus enough posts to place at intervals of 5 feet or less in between.

In place of a gate, you can simply hook the mesh to the house at one end of the fence, or to a wood post. Attach a 4-foot 2 by 4 vertically to the house wall. Near the top, bottom, and center of the edge facing away from the play yard, screw in 2- by ³⁄₁₆-inch screw hooks.

For more convenience, connect the mesh to an existing fence and gate.

How to build. Below are instructions for putting up one run of fencing. To fence in the entire play yard, simply repeat the steps for the remaining runs.

1. Start with one end of the fence. For extra rigidity, try to nail the fence to one corner of the house or a sturdy wood post attached to the house framing. If the layout of your house and yard won't permit this kind of anchoring, position the first metal post, facing the wire-holding prongs toward the play yard interior; drive the post 12 inches into the soil, using a sledgehammer. Check the post occasionally with a level for plumb.

2. Drive another post into the soil at the run's opposite end. To establish a straight line for the intermediate posts, tightly stretch twine between the two posts and tie firmly. Plan to add intermediate posts at evenly spaced intervals of 5 feet or less.

3. Measuring from the first post, drive the additional posts 12 inches into the ground. Align them with the twine and keep them plumb.

4. To strengthen the corner, drive another post at a right angle to the end post of the previous run.

5. Unroll the wire fencing on the ground on the inside of the posts; flatten it out. With a helper, lift one end of the mesh to one of the corner posts and hook it onto the wire-holding prongs (or nail one end to a house corner as shown below at left). If necessary, slightly bend out the prongs with a screwdriver (see below at center). To hook the mesh onto the bottom prongs, which are turned downward, you may have to bend the mesh slightly.

6. Pull the mesh tight; then hook it onto the next post. Continue along the entire run. At the last post, cut off the excess with wire cutters, snipping off any protruding wires.

Bind together any paired corner posts with wire, as shown below, and snip off protruding ends.

Nail mesh fence to house.

Using a screwdriver, bend out prongs.

Bind posts together with wire.

Getting in Gear

Choosing & using baby equipment

For a creature so small, a baby usually requires an amazing quantity of supplies. The list may start with a few dozen diapers, but it soon moves on to such larger items as a crib, stroller, high chair, and playpen. The safe design and use of these kinds of gear, and more, are discussed in this chapter. Two safety rules apply to them all: first, always purchase items from a reputable retailer; second, try them out before you buy to be sure they fit your child and you know how to use them correctly.

The U.S. Consumer Product Safety Commission (CPSC), a federal agency founded in 1973, regulates the manufacture of cribs and portable wooden-slat cribs. Any *new* one you buy today will meet its safety regulations.

Potentially hazardous products for which there are no specific federal safety standards may have been individually checked by the CPSC, but usually only after complaints have been filed. Also, certain parts or details of gear—such as scissorlike hardware—are banned by federal law.

Children's gear manufacturers also regulate themselves voluntarily through organizations such as the Juvenile Products Manufacturers Association (JPMA). It issues a "Certified" seal that states that a product has met voluntary standards under the guidelines of the American Society for Testing and Materials.

To date, JPMA has certified high chairs, playpens, strollers, carriages, walkers, and gates and is developing certification for other products.

Car seats (child restraining devices, or CRDs) are regulated by the National Highway Traffic Safety Administration. All car seats manufactured after January 1, 1981, must meet government standards.

Some toys are governed by CPSC regulations. Many other toys are produced in accordance with voluntary standards endorsed by an industry association, the Toy Manufacturers of America, Inc. (TMA).

Sleeping Gear

A baby's bed serves as a cozy home for both sleep and play.

By far the favorite bed for today's baby is the crib: it's convenient, practical, and comfortable up to about the age of 2½.

And, because it comes under federal safety regulations (which were first enacted in 1974), it is generally the safest baby bed.

Crib specifications

Check the crib you plan to use to be sure it has the following safety features. Be cautious with a second-hand or custom-made crib.

■ Crib slats must be spaced no wider apart than 2⅜ inches.

Some babies' bodies can slip between wider spaces.

■ Be sure crib end panels (or headboards) don't have decorative cutouts that might entrap a baby's head or other body part.

■ To prevent babies from falling out, the distance from the mattress support in its lowest position to the top of the end panels or rails in their highest position should be at least 26 inches. The minimum safe distance from the mattress support in its highest position to the top of the drop side in its lowest position is 9 inches.

■ Avoid cribs with corner posts, even if less than an inch high. These can catch children's clothing or anything that might be around a child's neck.

■ Interior dimensions should be between 51¾ and 53 inches long and 27⅜ and 28⅝ inches wide.

■ Make sure that the crib mattress fits snugly. Check that no more than two fingers can fit between the crib and mattress. (Babies have become trapped in these spaces, even suffocating as a result.)

■ The latching mechanisms or locks that release the drop side should be well out of baby's

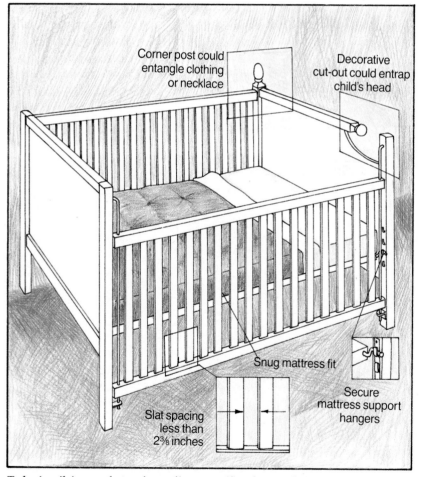

Corner post could entangle clothing or necklace

Decorative cut-out could entrap child's head

Snug mattress fit

Secure mattress support hangers

Slat spacing less than 2⅜ inches

Today's crib is manufactured according to specific safety regulations issued by the Consumer Product Safety Commission.

reach and require dual action for release, or at least 10 pounds of force. All hardware should be safe and free of sharp edges.

Second-hand cribs

Besides making sure that a second-hand crib meets the specifications on the facing page, check that it's in good working condition and that no parts are missing. Cribs painted before 1978, when legislation went into effect to limit lead in paints, should be stripped and refinished. Use high-quality, nontoxic household enamel on a clean, smooth surface (to prevent chipping) and allow to dry completely (to dispel toxic vapors). Also remove any decorative decals or stickers that come on a second-hand crib.

Safe crib use

Always lock crib rails in their upright position when baby is in the crib and unattended.

Be sure to remove the plastic wrapping from the mattress and any other parts; tie it in knots and discard in the outdoor trash. Never use plastic bags as mattress covers, because the clinging film can suffocate babies.

Until baby can stand, line the crib interior with bumper pads that tie or snap in place with at least six straps. When baby can stand, remove the pads so they can't be used for climbing out. Also remove large toys that could be used for the same purpose and lower the mattress to its lowest position. A child who is 35 inches tall has outgrown safe use of the crib and should graduate to a lower toddler's bed.

Keep the crib free and clear of long ribbons, cords, hanging toys, and mobiles. Industry standards recommend that all crib or playpen toys have strings no longer than 12 inches, as well as a label that cautions against use after the age of 5 months or when a baby can push up on hands and knees. (At this point, entanglement is more likely.)

Other baby beds

Cradles, bassinets, and portable beds are popular alternatives to cribs for the first few months of life.

Cradles. For safety, their rockers should curve only slightly, making a gentle motion. Cradles are not completely regulated, so look for the safety features outlined below.

Choose the highest sides possible to prevent baby from tumbling out. On a suspended cradle, check for a wide, sturdy base, secure pivoting hardware, and a design that lets you lock the cradle in a nonswinging position. No matter what design you choose, discontinue use of the cradle at 3 months or when your baby can raise up.

Wicker bassinets. Also not regulated completely, bassinets—like cradles—are safe to use only for newborns under 3 months. Make sure that the lining is securely attached and free of ribbons or buttons and that there are no loose, protruding reeds. If the bassinet is second-hand, look it over carefully, following the guidelines for second-hand cribs.

Portable cribs. Measure to make sure that the distance from the mattress support in its lowest position to the top of the side in its highest position is at least 22 inches.

Make sure that any folding hardware locks securely before use and cannot collapse.

Remember that a portable crib or bassinet is not meant for transporting a baby in the car. It is not a safe substitute for an up-to-date car seat (see page 67).

A cradle to rock your baby (in the first 3 months) should have high sides and a wide, stable base.

Mealtime Gear

From booster seats to feeding tables, a variety of dining furniture is available for today's young child. By far the most popular choice—though not always the safest—is the high chair.

High chair checklist

To a parent, the high chair is a wonderful convenience. It seats baby at an adult level, yet restrains wriggling and mess-making.

To the small child, a high chair looks like an indoor climbing gym. The more agile the tot, the more strain on the high chair's safety straps, tray lock, and stability of construction. Unfortunately, many kids, when standing, reaching, climbing, or just rocking, fall from high chairs or cause them to topple.

How can you prevent these accidents? Choose safe equipment and use it properly. For assurance of high standards, look for the JPMA "Certified" seal.

■ A reasonably safe high chair can hold 50 to 100 pounds. Check that all surfaces are free of sharp edges or protrusions, as well as hardware that could pinch or cut.

■ Be sure the chair comes with a sturdy safety belt with a crotch strap that's not attached to the tray and is easy to use, even when you're in a hurry. The tray may not be a safe restraint on its own: always strap in your child immediately after seating.

■ Choose a high chair with a locking tray that your child can't push off. Before buying a high chair, try it out to see how easily you can remove, replace, adjust, or lock its tray with one hand. A good design swings or slides out without detaching from the chair. The tray should also be unbreakable if dropped.

■ The high chair's base should be wide enough for good stability against tipping, even when your child rocks back and forth.

■ Make sure that a folding high chair locks securely when in use that the tray is locked in place after you seat your child.

■ Don't allow your toddler to climb the high chair. Keep the high chair a safe distance away from the stove, other kitchen equipment, family traffic, and places where the little one could push off against a wall or counter.

■ Keep an eye on your child while in the high chair. It's not safe to leave him or her unattended.

Other chairs

Although high chairs have remained the standard item for many years, alternative chairs are available that seat small children at a lower level.

Feeding tables provide secure seating for both mealtime and play. Set up close to floor level, they resemble walkers, except that most tables don't have wheels. From the time a child can sit up until about age 2, the feeding table offers all the advantages of a high chair with less risk of falling.

As with a high chair, place a feeding table away from dangerous areas and objects. Look for a feeding table tray that's too wide for your child to reach across.

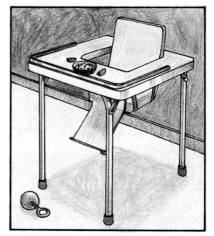

Feeding tables are safer than high chairs because they're lower. If you choose a model with wheels, make sure that they lock in a stationary position.

A feeding table should be well built and should fit your child comfortably. It should have a safety strap with a crotch strap to keep the little one from wriggling or sliding out; check to see that you can fasten the strap easily.

If the feeding table is a fold-up design, make sure that its locking device holds securely in the open position. Don't leave your child unattended while in a feeding table.

Booster seats are popular dining chair accessories for toddlers. Used at home or in public, the booster seat is safe if used properly.

Belt the booster seat to the chair; then strap your child to the booster seat. Your child should be at least 18 months old and able to sit up straight with good balance.

Use only a sturdy, flat-seated, straight-backed chair as a base. Do not leave the child unattended in a booster seat.

Hook-on chairs attach to the edge of the dining table. Also called hanging chairs, they're simple and portable, and they invite an older baby or young child to join the family at the table. Most will hold a child up to about 40 pounds.

But the best-designed hook-on chair's safety depends on how securely you attach it, as well as whether your table can support the chair and the child's weight and remain stable.

Buy only a chair with a clamp that locks onto the table. Test the chair's attachment by putting weight on it.

Check that caps or plugs on tubing are firmly fixed and cannot be pulled loose by your child.

Make sure the chair has a safety belt—and use it. Also be sure that there's no other chair or any object nearby from which the seated child could push off with the feet.

Dining in style for today's child can mean anything from a traditional oak high chair to a more contemporary design. But safety features remain constant—and more important than fashionable appearance.

Gear on the Go

Ahhh...sweet freedom! Strollers, backpacks, and infant carriers pave the way for you to get out in the fresh air with your baby. While your little one experiences all the sights, sounds, and sensations of the outside world, you're free to shop, walk, work, or chat with a neighbor.

Back indoors again, your baby may enjoy more roving about in a walker. Keep a close eye on the little wanderer.

Strollers

For walks to the park or mornings at the shopping mall, a stroller can become almost as essential as the family car. It lets baby lounge in comfort, and it frees a parent from lifting and carrying.

A stroller that reclines completely and is well protected by a canopy can carry newborns. Otherwise, when your baby is about 3 months, start using a canopied stroller that supports the infant in a semi-reclining position. Many parents continue to use the stroller for tired kids up to about age 4.

In 1983, JPMA developed a voluntary program for certification of strollers. Look for their certification seal and these safety features in picking out a stroller:

■ It must have a wide wheel base to guard against tipping, even when your child leans far over one side or reclines backward.

■ Choose large wheels or sets of double wheels that help stabilize the stroller. Models with swiveling wheels give a smoother ride.

■ Make sure that the seat belt is durable, for it will get hard use for several years. Is it easy to use? If not, you may not bother with it. But, to be safe, you must fasten it whenever you seat your child in the stroller.

■ Test the brake to be sure that it's easy to find and operate in a hurry and that it locks the wheels securely. Don't leave your child unattended in a stroller, no matter how good its brakes are.

■ The basket for carrying supplies should be mounted low on

Have you ever been greeted by a grinning baby in a backpack while waiting in line at the store or bank? Besides being fun for baby, a backpack offers extra safety in a crowd.

the back of the stroller, in front of or directly over the rear wheels. Otherwise, its extra weight when filled could tip the stroller.

Baby carriers

We're a mobile society, so it's not surprising that we enjoy a variety of excellent designs for moving our young along with us. Backpacks, front packs, and infant "carrier" seats have become almost standard equipment for recently born Americans. Largely, their safety depends on careful use of the carrier.

Front packs, designed to keep young babies snug and safe against the fronts of their parents, stay useful until the baby weighs about 15 pounds. Choose a front pack that gives good head and neck support, especially if your baby is under 3 months. While you're carrying the baby this way, it's unsafe to do anything that you wouldn't do if you were holding the baby in your arms. If you have any kind of back trouble, a front pack may aggravate it (a backpack may prove easier).

Backpacks are intended for older, bigger babies. Make sure that leg openings are neither too small nor too large (big enough to slip through) for your youngster. The pack should also fit you comfortably. Make sure it has a well-padded edge wherever your baby might bump. Choose a pack that's easy to take off with minimal risk of accidentally dropping it (there are models that stand on their own). There should be a waist strap to help distribute the weight evenly.

As you carry your baby in a backpack, be sure that he or she is seated deep inside it, with the back fully supported. Bend from the knees—not the waist—while wearing the pack to lessen the risk of your baby falling out (it's easier on the back, too).

Infant carriers come in varied designs, from a plastic lounge chair to a more entertaining bouncing sling of fabric stretched over a metal frame. Unless used carelessly by adults, carriers can be safe, convenient, and fun.

Make sure that your baby is the right size for the seat, usually under 16 to 20 pounds (follow the manufacturer's guideline). Make sure that the carrier or bounce seat has a wide, stable base. Test to be sure the base won't skid as your baby wriggles. If the seat has a metal support that snaps into its back, make sure that it locks securely and won't pop out.

These chairs must have easy-to-use seat belts. Always strap your baby in. In a bounce chair, without a seat belt, the baby could propel right out.

Always place the seat where there is no chance of baby toppling over an edge or pushing off with its feet. A tabletop is not safe unless you are sitting right next to your child. Never consider these seats as babysitters, even briefly, and *never consider them a safe substitute for a car seat.*

Walkers—are they safe?

Baby walkers are much loved by some parents and their small offspring. But other parents and some pediatricians consider walkers unsafe.

Simple umbrella style at left costs much less than the deluxe model at right. Does the higher price buy more safety? Not necessarily: both strollers are well constructed for safe riding.

The main problem is that walkers sometimes tip over and, in a moment of carelessness, they can even roll perilously down a flight of stairs.

In conjunction with the CPSC, the JPMA has sponsored voluntary certification standards for walkers. Also, the CPSC has banned the most hazardous aspects of walker design. If you decide to have a walker at home, follow these safety guidelines:

■ Make sure that the walker has no scissoring, shearing, or pinching hinges, springs, or other hardware accessible to your child. There must be no holes (or slots) larger than ⅛ inch in which a finger could get trapped. Make sure that the walker won't collapse accidentally while in use.

■ Make sure that its base is wide enough to prevent tipping and that the walker is wide enough to block a baby's reach to objects on either side. Are the wheels large enough to minimize the risk of tipping? Are they securely attached to the frame?

■ For safe riding, keep the walker on the ground floor, blocked off from dangerous areas, such as the front door. Remove throw rugs, which can cause a walker to tip over. Most important of all, stay close by while your baby is in the walker.

Playpens & Safety Gates

Small children are notorious for mishaps, often caused by their eagerness to explore. They lack a sense of danger at a time when they're gaining new physical skills every day.

To keep your little bundle of curiosity off the stairs, you'll probably want to buy a safety gate. And a playpen is a big help, too, at times.

Choosing a playpen

Also called a play yard, the playpen offers a safe place for baby to play and, as a result, a short respite for exhausted parents.

For assurance of high standards, look for the JPMA "Certified" seal.

Playpens are generally meant for children no taller than 34 inches, no heavier than 30 pounds, and under the age of about 2. Look for these other safety factors:

■ Many mesh playpens are designed so that one side drops down (making it easier to lift the child in or out). *Never leave the side dropped down while your baby is in the playpen.* It can entrap and even suffocate a small child. For added safety, choose a mesh playpen designed without a drop side.

■ Make sure that the support structures are well protected. If wood, the top rail should have a sturdy plastic teething edge. Also check all edges to be sure that they're smooth and rounded. Check that hinges and other hardware can't cause injury.

■ A well-designed playpen should be at least 20 inches high, from its base to the top of its sides. Wood bars should be spaced no wider than 2⅜ inches, and mesh openings should be no bigger than ¼ inch.

■ Sharp hardware should be covered by caps or plugs that a child cannot remove. The playpen should have sturdy locks to prevent a child from lowering or collapsing it.

■ Like baby gates of similar design, accordion-style playpens have caused enough accidents that the CPSC now warns that older types are unsafe because they have openings large enough to entrap a small child's head.

Safe playpen use

Much like a baby's crib, the playpen is a safe sleep-and-play space if well designed. Even so, parents need to follow many of the same

A playpen is a safe, padded parking place for baby when you need to answer the phone or turn your back for a few minutes.

safe-use practices as given for cribs (see page 57).

To foil climbing out, remove bumper pads and large toys once your child can stand up. Another crib rule that also applies to the playpen: *Do not strap crib toys* across the top of the playpen or along its sides after your baby is 5 months old or can raise up on hands and knees.

Be careful not to place the playpen near a window, a radiator, a fireplace in use, or dangerous objects that the baby might reach.

Check the playpen's condition occasionally. Is the mesh intact or unraveling? Is the fabric or vinyl rail-covering intact, or is there a chance that your teething baby might choke on chewed-off pieces?

Child safety gates

Several styles of baby gates are available for blocking children at an open doorway, at stairs, or in a hallway. They range from about 24 to 32 inches in height; most can be adjusted to various door widths up to about 42 inches. For very wide openings, you can get a wooden bar gate that will expand to 8 feet (see page 39). The typical minimum width that gates will fit is 27 inches; one model will compress to 22 inches.

Some gates are pressure-mounted between walls or door jambs; they are very easy to install. Others have a fixed (often hinged) attachment at one or both sides; these are generally more secure for blocking off stairs or where an extra measure of security counts. Choose a baby gate that is easy for adults to open and close so it will be used consistently.

Do not use older accordion-style gates that can entrap a child's head. Even though the CPSC has found these to be dangerous, many are still passed around or sold second-hand.

Newer designs with openings no bigger than 2⅜ inches are safer.

Baby gates are certified by JPMA. Look for their "Certified" seal. Here are a few important rules for buying and using safety gates:

■ The gate's construction should be free of sharp or pointed hardware and areas that can entrap a child. Minimum spacing between bars should be 2⅜ inches. Make sure that your child cannot climb over the gate.

■ The latching mechanism should work effectively, consistently, and easily (for you).

■ The gate should be mounted according to the manufacturer's instructions. Assure yourself that the mounting is secure.

■ The gate is not a substitute for your attentiveness. Be watchful; don't rely completely on the gate to contain your child who, at one time or another, may learn how to get over or around it.

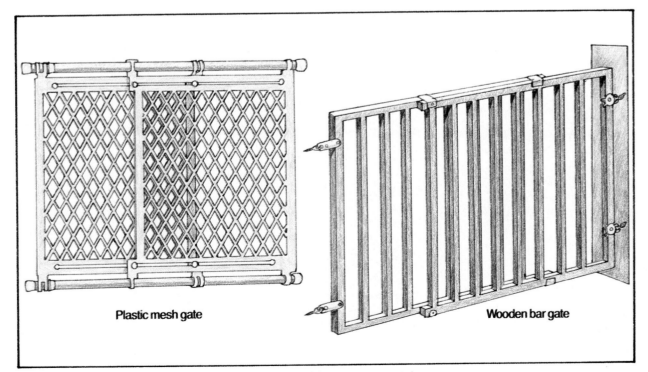

Plastic mesh gate

Wooden bar gate

Safety gates are available in several styles and sizes. Gate at left is pressure-mounted in a doorway; gate at right is screwed in at one side, latched at the other.

Choosing Safe Toys

Toys make learning fun, and the favorite ones get hard use. When buying a toy, parents usually consider whether their child will like it and learn from it—and how long it will last. At the same time, however, it makes sense to question the toy's safety.

Fortunately, most of today's American-made toys are quite safe if played with as the manufacturer directs. Most have been constructed according to safety criteria established by the TMA or the CPSC.

Always check toys and packaging for other descriptive or cautionary labels. On electric toys (for children older than 8 years), look for a UL (Underwriters Laboratory) mark. By law, painted toys must have nontoxic finishes.

Age guidelines

You wouldn't give a baby a jigsaw puzzle, because a baby would probably chew—and possibly choke—on the tiny pieces. A basic rule of toy safety is to make sure that toys are appropriate for the age and maturity level of the child who plays with them.

Today's toy manufacturers label toys with appropriate age ranges for their products. Read and follow these age recommendations.

Toys to avoid

Certain imported toys, old or broken ones, as well as toys designed for older children can all pose dangers for the young and inexperienced. And not all manufacturers adhere to the standards set by the TMA, which are purely voluntary.

Older siblings' toys and other older kids' possessions need to be kept away from small children. Who wants a 3-year-old to run wild with a baseball bat?

Cords, strings, and ribbons that might end up wrapped around a baby's neck add nothing but potential trouble to a toy. Shorten the cord of your child's innocent-looking toy telephone so that it's less than 10 inches long.

Small toy parts can be swallowed by a tot, cause choking, or become lodged in the ear or nose. A CPSC regulation bans small parts in toys manufactured for children under age 3. The ban covers such things as squeakers in squeeze toys and removable eyes and noses in stuffed animals and dolls. Baby rattles must be large enough that they can't

become lodged in a baby's throat and constructed so that they won't separate into smaller pieces.

Check older toys carefully for sturdy construction and good, solid condition. Make sure that no small parts or stuffing could come loose.

Balloons are not safe for small children to play with unless you closely supervise. Bits of small rubber from popped balloons can block a youngster's air passage.

Points, sharp edges, and projectiles—it goes without saying—could cause harm to kids at any age. Be especially watchful for toys that break, exposing sharp edges.

Pacifiers occasionally come apart or are small enough for a baby to choke on; choose one with care. Discard it as soon as it looks worn. Never tie a pacifier or put any kind of necklace around a baby's neck.

Electrical toys, usually labeled for use only by kids older than 8, require caution and your super-

Choosing safe toys *for your kids is easy when you're presented with today's colorful abundance of excellent designs that are sturdy, lightweight, unbreakable, nontoxic, and free of small parts.*

vision. Also note that aluminized polyester film kites (now banned by the CPSC) and balloons pose the risk of electrocution should they contact power lines.

Putting toys away

For their own peace of mind, most parents teach young chil-dren to put away toys after play. It's also a good safety habit, because it cuts down the chances of stumbling over toys, as well as breaking them. Wheeled toys on or near a staircase can cause a serious accident.

For storing toys, consider lightweight open boxes or bas-kets of plastic. Often they stack neatly and they usually come in bright colors. Small children can maneuver them without coming to any harm.

Traditional toy chests are less safe, especially if they have a lid (see page 23).

If toys break, take them away—either to securely mend or discard.

Safety in the Car

We're all so familiar with the family car—our home-away-from-home—that we don't usually think of it as dangerous.

Yet, the tragic truth is that car collisions claim more children's lives than any other kind of accident, and more than all childhood diseases. However, good protection in a car can make a big difference to a passenger's safety at any age.

Seat belt protection

Kids look to their parents as role models. To give your young ones an example of safety, *always buckle up your seat belt when in a moving car.*

Babies and small children, as explained below, need both seat belts and car seats to protect them. And older children need to practice good seat belt habits, just as adults do. They will be safest in the back seat. If it has only lap belts, the belt should fit snugly across the hips (not at lap level). If necessary, three children can share two seat belts, as shown on page 68.

In general, for passengers of all ages, a lap-shoulder combination seat belt provides much better protection than a lap-only belt. Make sure that the shoulder strap fits snugly across the shoulder; on a child, if it crosses the face and neck, tuck it behind the child's back. Never hook it under an arm.

When a mother-to-be fastens her seat belt, she greatly reduces the risk of harm not only to herself but to her unborn baby as well, according to the American College of Obstetricians and Gynecologists. Like anyone else, she should place the seat belt as low and pull it as tight as possible.

For safety, an infant-sized car seat is always installed so that it faces the rear of the car.

Also safe transport during the first year, this convertible car seat is shown in its infant position.

Unsafe rides

While in a moving car, it's unsafe to hold a baby or small child in your lap. In a collision, this could increase the chances of severe injury to the child.

More obviously dangerous is to let children of any age ride in the open bed of a pickup truck or in the back of a camper or motor home. The cargo area of a station wagon or van is not safe either.

Car seats

Throughout the United States today, car seats (or "child-restraining devices") are required by law for small children who are passengers in cars. The seats themselves must meet federal safety standards in effect since 1981. Look for labels indicating that they have been "Dynamically Crash Tested" and are certified for use in both cars and aircraft.

For a baby or child weighing under 40 pounds, *the most*

important protection that you can provide in a car is correct and regular use of an approved car seat. Be sure that your child will fit the seat, that the seat fits your car, and that you understand its installation and correct use before you buy it.

Choices and sizes. Car seats now come in three sizes, based on children's weights. For safety, it's important to *use the correct size.*

■ Infant seats, the least expensive but the soonest outgrown, carry babies home from the hospital and right on toward the end of their first year, or up to 18 to 20 pounds. Safety requires that seats made only for infants be firmly strapped so that they *face the rear of the car.*

■ Toddler (or preschool) car seats are designed for children from about 20 to 50 pounds but not for infants. These are strapped to face forward.

■ Convertible seats simplify life by seating children from

infant size through toddler size. As an infant car seat, the device is strapped to face the car's rear. For safety's sake, it does not fully recline. It should not be turned forward until the baby can sit up unaided and weighs at least 20 pounds.

■ Auto booster seats protect children who weigh between 30 and 60 pounds. Some models provide their own harnesses or shields against impact. The most effective booster seats have fully adjustable shields. Otherwise, use the car's seat belt, which should cross the boosted child's shoulder at about the position where it would cross an adult's.

Economical options. Some communities sponsor programs that loan or rent car seats at a low fee. Call the pediatric department of a local hospital to find such a program near you. Plan ahead in case of waiting lists.

If you buy or receive a used car seat, make sure that it's in good condition with no missing

Adjusted for toddlers, the convertible car seat shown on the facing page (at right) faces forward.

For children who weigh from 30 to 60 pounds, use an auto booster seat, safest with an adjustable shield.

…safety in the car

For seat belts that are designed to stay loose, it's important to add a locking clip for safe installation of your child's car seat.

parts. Look for the label on its back that gives the date of manufacture. The most reliable seats have been made since January 1, 1981, when federal safety standards were implemented. Make sure, too, that the car seat comes with the original manufacturer's instructions, or you may not be able to install or use it correctly.

If a used or borrowed car seat has been involved in a car accident, do not consider it safe.

Installation tips. Car seats are usually safer in the back seat. But if you find yourself watching your baby in the rearview mirror, the front seat is safer.

Note that some seat belts are designed to stay loose until a sudden stop makes them lock. This kind of seat belt cannot safely secure a car seat unless you buy a locking clip, usually available where car seats are sold or

from auto dealers. Use it as shown at left.

Follow the car seat manufacturer's instructions explicitly. By law, these are now printed right on the seat. When the seat is strapped in, pull on it to test how tightly it is secured.

Other car safety measures

Beyond the basics of car seats and seat belts, here are a few more tips for safer, happier driving:
■ Lock car doors. ■ Test that seat belts and car seat parts are cool before they touch your child. ■ Never leave a child unattended in the car. ■ Give children a few soft toys and lightweight books, but keep hard objects away from them and off the car's dashboard or rear window ledge. ■ Allow no rough play or hanging out the windows. ■ Make stops on trips to rest and stretch.

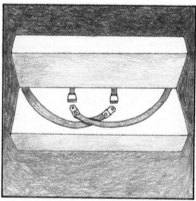

Three kids in the back seat can share two adult-size seat belts. It's far from the safest way to buckle up, but better than no seat belts at all. As shown above, the left belt stretches to the right buckle, and the right belt to the left buckle; this creates a "belt" for the center child.

BIKE SAFETY

Whether riding on the back of a parent's bike or pedaling one of their own, most children love the experience. And for some families, the bike may be the most practical mode of transport.

Be aware that in some states bike seats for children are not considered safe and have been banned.

Kids as passengers

When you do take your young child along on a bike, ride only on quiet streets, on bike paths, and in parks. Ride at slow speeds, allowing extra time to brake. Go only in good weather and full daylight.

■ Before their first birthday, babies are too young to ride as bike passengers.

■ Carry tots from 1 to 4 years (no more than 40 pounds) in a bike seat, such as the one shown at right, that protects their feet and hands from the bike's spokes.

■ Make sure that the seat is correctly installed. Also install a spoke guard. Try out the child in the seat to be sure there's no chance of falling.

■ Be sure to belt the child into the seat. Both you and the child should wear helmets.

Kids as cyclists

As the first safety checkpoint, look over your child's bike. Is it in good working condition? And is it the right size for your son or daughter? If it's the right size, your child will be able to hold onto the handlebars while sitting

Before a bike ride through the park, father and son gear up for safety: helmets for both, a securely installed child's bike seat, and a spoke guard for extra protection.

on the seat and touch the balls of both feet on the ground at the same time. While standing on the ground over the bike, your child should clear the bike's cross bar with at least 1 inch between crotch and crossbar.

Next, check out how well your child can ride. For safety's sake, be sure your young cyclist can do the following:

■ Squeeze both hand brakes at once to stop the bike.

■ Ride in a relatively straight line.

■ Stop quickly and get off without falling.

Once you're confident of your child's ability on the bike, it's also important to teach basic biking safety:

■ Stop at all intersections and watch for traffic.

■ Follow all traffic rules. Obey lights, ride to the right side, and stop at stop signs.

■ Ride only in daylight, not during or after dusk.

■ Wear a helmet and bright clothes that are easy for drivers to see.

■ Don't ride "double" or on a borrowed bike.

Family Safety Handbook

How to handle emergencies

Beyond baby's safety gate lies a big, wide, often unsafe world outside the home. Kids quickly and eagerly discover it. But for years, they will rely on adults to teach them how to stay reasonably safe in it.

You can't childproof the whole world for your little one, or even make your home 100 percent child-proof. But much serious harm can be avoided simply through safety awareness, planning, and good habits. Serious consequences can be reduced, too, if you know how to handle an emergency.

The following pages point out many ways that you can steer a safe course for yourself and your youngsters. This chapter covers the basics of home fire safety, including information on smoke detectors, fire extinguishers, and escape ladders. For other kinds of disaster, too, being prepared can make a crucial difference.

To complete your readiness, we recommend learning cardio-pulmonary resuscitation (CPR) and other first aid techniques from a community class. Check with your local American Red Cross chapter or public health department to find such a class nearby.

Another safety concern covered here is how to find the right babysitter for your son or daughter. Babysitters themselves need their own safety guidelines so they can know what to do in an emergency. This chapter includes a checklist for them.

Your kids are sure to ask questions about safety, and the answers should prove helpful to them. But usually a more lasting impression is made by what parents teach by such examples as fastening seat belts or putting away tools after use.

Fire Safety Tips

Big, loud fire trucks thrill young children—and parents, too, as long as the trucks' destination is far from home. None of us wants to see our own house go up in flames, nor to believe that it could.

Yet carelessness and ignorance about fire safety turn homes into tinderboxes every day. The good news is that smoke detectors (see facing page), when correctly installed and used, now save many lives and homes that once would have been destroyed by fire.

Electrical fire hazards

One of the most frequent causes of house fires is electricity used carelessly or incorrectly. Check your own home for these hazards:

■ Outlet "extenders," or "cube taps," which overload electrical circuits

■ Wrong size fuse substituted for a blown fuse

■ Extension or other electrical cords that are frayed, have broken wires, or have brittle, worn insulation; replace them, don't repair them

■ Receptacles and appliances that are not properly grounded; if your older home doesn't have three-hole grounding receptacles, either upgrade its wiring or have an electrician check that

your appliances are properly grounded, double insulated, or polarized (the last option requires polarized receptacles as well)

■ Extension cords that are not matched to the wattage of the appliance plugged into them

■ Too many appliances plugged into an extension cord, which can overload the circuit

■ Bulbs in light fixtures that exceed the fixture's wattage limit (if you don't know the limit, use no more than 60-watt bulbs); recessed fixtures can be especially hazardous because of heat buildup

Heat & combustibles

Accidental fires can start if combustible materials too close to a fireplace, stove, or heater overheat. Consider these points:

■ Many furnishings, draperies, and carpets are fire-resistant. Make sure that all of yours are.

■ Keep combustibles, such as trash, newspapers, and rags, to a minimum. Keep any combustible material (including upholstery, curtains, and rugs) safely away from your water heater, fireplace, furnace, gas dryer, or any appliance that heats up.

■ *Portable electric space heaters can be very dangerous,* especially around children. If tipped over, the heater can start a fire unless it has a safety switch that automatically shuts it off. Make sure that yours has a UL (Underwriters

Laboratory) mark, which ensures the presence of such a switch.

Electric-element heaters get very hot. The grills of some models have spaces that are wide enough to allow small fingers to reach the element. Look for the UL mark as assurance of safe grill design—but also make sure that your child cannot get near the heater or its cord.

■ Kerosene heaters are extremely hazardous if not adequately vented. Besides creating indoor pollution (see page 76), they also pose a great fire hazard if tipped over.

■ Make sure that your fireplace has a secure screen to stop sparks from flying out of the fire.

■ Make sure that installation of your woodstove or fireplace meets local building code specifications. Keep combustibles well away from either.

■ Chimneys for a wood stove or fireplace should be properly installed. If there's no spark arrestor on the chimney cap, install one. Keep chimneys clean: a buildup of creosote on the fireplace inner walls (or wood stove chimney) can ignite during a hot fire. Help to prevent this with annual chimney cleaning and inspection. Have a mason inspect the chimney's mortar and bricks.

SMOKE DETECTORS

Most fatal home fires occur at night, while unaware victims sleep. Such tragedies point up the value of installing smoke detectors in your home. These devices will react to smoke and sound a shrill alarm. (Note that heat detectors are not nearly as sensitive as smoke detectors.)

Because they sound during the early stages of a fire, smoke detectors give you the few extra minutes needed to escape before a fire spreads.

To back up the smoke detectors, you might consider installing a home sprinkler system. Sensitive to heat, these activate automatically in response to a sudden blaze.

Types of detectors

Smoke detectors sense smoke either through ionization or through a photoelectric cell. The most common types use the ionization principle, which causes combustion products to interfere with the flow of electric current in the detector, setting off the alarm. Such detectors are generally considered slightly more sensitive and quicker to respond to hot-flame fires than photoelectric smoke detectors.

One problem with ionization detectors is that they react to extreme changes in humidity or temperature. When used near kitchens or bathrooms, they frequently go off if exposed to steam. In these areas, photoelectric smoke detectors make more sense.

Where to put detectors

For good protection, place a smoke detector on each level of your home and outside each sleeping area (one detector in the hallway can serve all bedrooms at that end of the hall if it's within 10 feet of the doors). *Sleep with bedroom doors closed, letting the smoke detector act as a sentinel outside.* If you smoke in the bedroom or have any other fire hazard there, place another smoke detector in the room.

In addition, you can put smoke detectors in the kitchen, living room, and anywhere else in the house or in outdoor buildings where there's a danger of fire. But don't use ionization smoke detectors within 20 feet of kitchens, garages, furnaces, or water heaters; in dusty or dirty areas; or within 10 feet of bathrooms. Neither kind of detector will function correctly near drafty areas, kitchen air streams, or air-conditioning or heating registers.

Mount detectors according to the manufacturer's directions, paying special attention to recommended clearances and setbacks from walls and corners.

Maintenance & testing

According to the National Fire Protection Association, it's estimated that from 25 to 33 percent of the smoke detectors installed in the United States are not working properly. Smoke and heat detectors are effective only if they are maintained and tested regularly (as shown at right).

If you own battery-operated detectors, you'll need to replace the batteries every year or before they run down. Almost all devices give off a trouble signal (a periodic beep) lasting 7 days when the charge is running low. Replace batteries immediately if the detector begins to beep. Test detectors regularly by pressing the test button. On a UL-marked detector, this will work reliably. To keep a detector clean, vacuum it once a month according to the manufacturer's instructions.

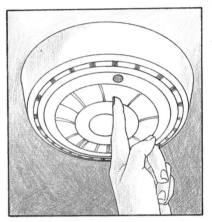

Smoke detectors should be tested monthly, when you clean them. On a UL-marked smoke detector, you can rely on the built-in testing button.

One final note: No detector has a perfect record for sensing fires. Be sure family members are familiar with fire-safety precautions.

...fire safety tips

Other common fire hazards

Everyday activities may start fires that quickly get out of hand.

Smoking materials cause many fires. Be sure to completely extinguish cigarettes and matches. After parties, check upholstered furniture and carpets for smoldering cigarette butts. *Never smoke in bed.* The fires from smoldering cushions and mattresses are especially pernicious, since you're not likely to notice them until they're out of control.

Matches, obviously, are not safe for children to play with (you may want to teach older kids how to strike them safely under your supervision). Keep matches, lighters, cigarettes, lighter fluid, lit candles, and incense well out of the reach of small children.

Grease on the kitchen stove, in the oven, or on the barbecue is a common fire hazard; keep it cleaned up.

At the kitchen range, loose sleeves easily catch fire; so do dish towels used as pot holders. Wear trim-fitting clothes and use pot holders designed for the purpose.

Hot appliances, such as an iron or curling iron, can start fires if not unplugged immediately after use.

Snuffing out small fires

If a fire of any size flares up, your first job is to get everyone out of danger.

Still, there are occasional small fires that can easily be extinguished before they turn into disasters.

Stop, drop, and roll is a survival rule to teach your kids (and the whole family) in case clothing ever catches fire. Rolling snuffs out the flames. Running, an instinctive response, only fans the flames, making them worse.

A kitchen grease fire in a pan is easily extinguished by placing a lid over the pan and turning off the range. Lack of oxygen snuffs out the fire. *Never try to put out a grease fire with water.* To put out an oven fire, just shut the door and turn off the heat.

Keep fire extinguishers handy in the kitchen, shop, garage, and furnace area, or wherever fire risks are highest in your home. Place the extinguisher near the exit to the area, out of a small child's reach but where it's easy for you to find. Know how to use the extinguisher so you don't have to stop to read directions in an emergency. *If a small fire starts, first get everyone out of danger; then use the extinguisher. But if a fire gets out of control, stop using the extinguisher and get everyone out of the house.*

Make sure that the extinguisher you buy has a UL mark. There are different kinds of fire extinguishers to handle different fires. A green **A** on the label indicates that the extinguisher will put out burning paper, wood, cloth, rubber, and many plastics.

Place a fire extinguisher near a room's exit, above small children's reach, and 6 feet or more from the probable source of blaze (the kitchen range, for example).

A red **B** means the extinguisher will work for flammable liquids such as kitchen greases, oils, gasoline, paints, and solvents. For electrical fires, you would look for a blue **C.** You can also buy a multipurpose dry-chemical extinguisher labeled **A-B-C** that will put out most kinds of fires.

Maintain an active charge in your extinguishers. Most fire departments will inspect fire extinguishers at no cost. Have them recharged if used even partially: look in the Yellow Pages under "Fire Extinguishers" or "Fire Equipment."

The family fire drill

Every member of the family can play a part in developing a family escape plan and in practicing in family fire drills. Everyone must know what escape route to take out of the house as soon as they hear the smoke alarm. Determine now who will take responsibility for little ones. Decide on and inform everyone of a nearby place to meet after leaving the house.

If the alarm goes off, evacuate the house quickly and calmly and call the fire department from a neighbor's house or call box. Make sure in advance that your house numbers are large and easily seen at night. *Do not go back into the burning building.*

For the escape route, if necessary in a bad fire, *each room should have two exits—such as a door and a window—*that even young members of the family can get through safely.

Provide a hook-on fire escape ladder (shown below) for each upper-story window required as a fire exit. (Such ladders are available at building supply stores.) Make sure that all adults and older children know how to

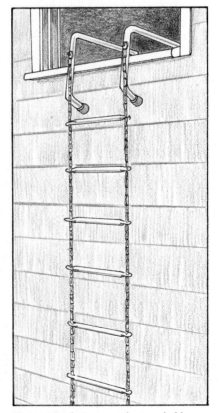

Two-story houses need escape ladders in case of fire. Make sure that parents and older children practice installing and climbing down the ladder.

HOLIDAY HAZARDS

Along with a lot of fun, holidays often mean disrupted routines, crowded parties, later bedtimes, excitement, and stress. These can add up to a greater likelihood of accidents, so be especially watchful of small children at such times.

And plan ahead for safe holidays. Enjoy a public fireworks display on the Fourth of July. With neighbors and other parents, organize a Halloween party. For preschoolers' birthdays, limit the guest list, so you don't end up with more 4-year-olds than you can safely handle. Invite other parents, too.

At Christmas, avoid a serious fire hazard by choosing the freshest available tree; cut it down yourself if possible. Keep it outdoors until it's time to trim it, and keep it in a water-filled stand throughout the holiday. Make sure lights have the UL mark. Take the tree down before it drops quantities of needles. Don't string lights on an artificial

metal tree because of the danger of electrical shock.

On any holiday, watch out that baby can't get into potentially harmful decorations or gift wrappings. Ornaments may be breakable or small enough to choke a child. Ribbons can get wrapped around the neck. Some materials may be toxic if baby tastes them.

Christmas is many children's favorite holiday. Keep it happy by practicing fire safety: a fresh tree and UL-marked lights in top condition.

install and climb down the ladder. Practice for familiarity. Keep it handy in a box below the window or under the bed.

Ahead of time, teach the family to *feel any interior door during the fire—then not to open it if it's hot.* Except for escape purposes, other doors and windows should be left closed (but don't take time to close them if they're open).

Teach the family to *escape on hands and knees* (where they will

breathe the freshest air) as soon as they smell smoke or hear the smoke alarm. Carbon monoxide poisoning is the number-one killer in fires. Tell your family that if trapped in smoke or fire, they should try to yell for help from a window.

A Safer Environment

Providing a healthy physical environment for your baby means more than safety gates and cuddly toys. It also means ensuring that no harmful microscopic particles or gases are contaminating the air in your home. And it means being prepared to cope with unexpected disasters in the world outside your front door.

Indoor pollution

Found not only in tainted lakes and urban smog, pollution also occurs in many homes, often insidiously, because it can be hard to detect.

Indoor air pollution problems have increased recently due to zealous energy conservation, especially in cold climates. Buttoning up a house tightly with insulation invites contamination to a degree unknown in drafty old houses with a plentiful circulation of fresh, outdoor air.

Luckily, most kinds of indoor pollution can be reversed by improved ventilation and cleanup, or by calling in expert help.

Household and personal care products—aerosol hair spray, laundry bleach, wet paint, and dozens of others—add their chemical taint to indoor air.

Besides keeping all such products out of children's reach, read the fine print on the products' labels. Follow manufacturer's directions to the letter. Use in areas of good ventilation and only when little ones are not underfoot.

Smoking pollutes indoor air. Small children are especially susceptible to "second-hand" smoke. Either allow no smoking in your home or at least reduce the pollution by using an air cleaner or exhaust fan, or by opening the windows.

Combustion emissions such as nitrogen dioxide and carbon monoxide are introduced into houses by poorly maintained and inadequately vented ranges, water heaters, dryers, and other gas appliances; fireplaces; unvented kerosene stoves; and wood or coal stoves. To prevent the same kind of pollution, *never leave a car or other gasoline engine running in a closed garage or shed.*

Make sure that your gas range has a hood fan or other exhaust fan that vents fumes outdoors. Never use a gas oven to heat your rooms. Have gas appliances and gas or oil furnaces inspected regularly by the local utility company. Convert to spark ignition in place of pilot lights, if possible. Check that all heaters are without cracks and are vented to the outside. Never cook with charcoal indoors. Be sure your fireplace or wood stove draws its combustion air from outdoors (through a special duct).

Asbestos, a group of noncombustible minerals with harmful fibers, was used in housing in the 1940s and 1950s in the form of fire-resistant ceiling and floor tiles, wallboard, and insulation around heating ducts. If your home was built since 1972, you're not likely to have this kind of problem. The material becomes hazardous when it crumbles, which releases the fibers.

Cover any exposed but intact asbestos completely with plastic and seal it with duct tape. *Do not try to remove it by yourself.* If you suspect loose asbestos, call your local building inspector or the nearest office of the Environmental Protection Agency (EPA) to get a referral for a professional cleanup.

Formaldehyde in homes—in large amounts—is usually found in the form of urea formaldehyde foam insulation. (Its use has been widespread.) It also exists in the resins of particleboard, fiber board, and plywood paneling— not usually posing problems unless hot and humid weather draws emissions from newly installed materials. It can come in some carpet, upholstery, and drapery fabrics, too.

Your best defense is plenty of fresh air. Improve circulation and install a good air cleaner (electronic ones are the most effective). Or block access to sources like particleboard with sealers and paint:

Other pollutants include common *bacteria and fungi* introduced by people and pets. Keep air conditioners, air ducts, humidifiers, dehumidifiers, and heat exchangers clean. Vacuum thoroughly.

Microwave ovens need regular cleaning, too. Do not use yours if it's not in top condition, especially if its door doesn't close tightly.

Radon gas, a radioactive gas given off by rocks and soil that contain traces of uranium or radium, has been found to be a severe pollutant in certain geographical areas. To inquire about local conditions and testing for radon, call the nearest field office of the EPA (also, the agency makes available a publication about radon).

Emergency preparedness

Every local environment poses its own kinds of potential disaster—tornadoes in Kansas, earthquakes in California, or crime in any city.

Look to community resources for ways to meet your particular environmental threats. Where crime rates are high, police departments usually offer expert advice on home security measures, as well as self-defense tactics away from home.

Contact public health agencies or the local chapter of the American Red Cross for specifics on how to prepare for a natural disaster, such as a hurricane or earthquake. As in preparing ahead in case of fire, teach everyone in the family what to do if disaster strikes— and have practice drills.

To deal with injuries, learn correct first aid techniques. Keep a fully supplied kit (see at right) both at home, out of small children's reach, and in the car.

FIRST AID SUPPLIES

Listed below are supplies that the American Red Cross recommends for a first aid kit. In many communities, the local chapter of this organization also sells (or can order) the kit shown below, designed for the car. Also available is a pamphlet on first aid. Complement these supplies by taking a class in first aid and cardio-pulmonary resuscitation (CPR) from your local American Red Cross chapter or other community resource.

- Sterilized gauze squares (assorted sizes)
- Roller gauze (one each of 1-inch, 2-inch, and 3-inch sizes)
- Eye pads
- Three triangular bandages
- Adhesive bandage packet
- Roll of adhesive tape (½- or 1-inch wide)
- Small scissors
- Tweezers
- One oral, one rectal thermometer
- Tongue blades and wooden applicator sticks
- Petroleum jelly or other lubricant
- Safety pins (assorted)
- Soap or other cleansing agent
- Any regularly taken, critical medication prescribed by your doctor
- Syrup of ipecac to induce vomiting (but to be used only in consultation with your doctor or poison control center)
- Copy of American Red Cross textbook *Standard First Aid & Personal Safety*

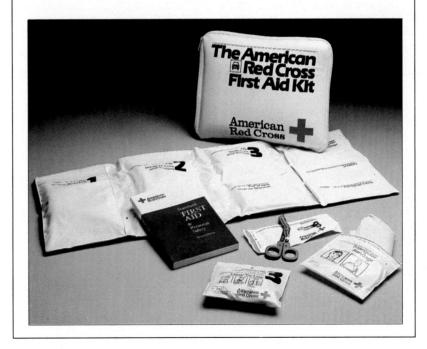

Out & About

From reorganizing closets to cleaning air, there are many ways to childproof a home.

But how do you childproof a big, bustling department store? What about the crowds at the carnival? And what can be done about grandma's white carpets and snarling Pekingese?

New horizons await you and your offspring as you venture out and about. Here are a few ways to keep your experiences as safe as possible.

On a visit

Whether you're visiting grandpa, grandma, auntie, or a friend, plan the trip in advance; this will save a lot of nervous wear-and-tear, as well as accidents.

Take along such childproofing equipment as outlet plugs (see page 10) and doorknob sleeves (see page 25) if you expect to be visiting for awhile.

Be observant and, with permission, clear surfaces of any small, breakable, or otherwise dangerous items that your child can reach. *For example, people who don't live with children are more apt to leave medications within easy reach.* Be sure to put everything back as you found it.

Also note locations of the telephone, electrical cords and appliances, stairs (it may be easiest to provide grandma with one or two safety gates), easily tipped furniture, and sharp edges, such as a glass tabletop. Look carefully for poisons, such as insecticides, that may be within your child's reach, both indoors and in the garden.

Often, on a visit, the safest approach is simply to keep your baby or toddler happy with comforts brought from home. For a long day, such as Thanksgiving, a playpen can help.

Teach children to be cautious toward unfamiliar dogs and cats, and never to go near the animal's food, even if it belongs to a beloved pet. (Note that pets can be trained not to snap at children.)

Coping in a crowd

In a crowd, if you don't keep your hand clasped to your 2- or 3-year-old, you could easily lose your child. Just in case, dress your little one in bright colors before going out.

Child-safe fun away from home, such as feeding ducks when out walking with Grandpa, is easy to find.

Available today (but not fool-proof) are electronic devices that help you track down wandering kids. Your son or daughter wears a small transmitter, and you keep a receiver that picks up its signal. There are also harnesses and wrist tethers to help cope at airports, department stores, or other crowded places. *Never leave your young child unattended in a shopping cart or elsewhere in public.*

Backpacks (see page 60) keep your baby or toddler safely with you at all times, and they also lift him or her above knee level for a more interesting view and greater protection. Strollers are less safe in a crowd, and they're a nuisance to take up an escalator or onto a bus (you must lift out and carry your child, managing the folded stroller with your other hand).

Babysitters

Sometimes it's the parents' turn to go out and about—once they've found a loving and reliable babysitter.

Whether a teenager or a senior citizen, the sitter you choose must be able to respond to any emergency calmly and effectively.

Before hiring sitters, check their references and consider past experience and any present health problems. Do you feel comfortable with the sitter? If not, your children probably won't.

Write out rules, routines, and the child's favorite foods, toys, and clothing. Explain any problems and medications (but try to give these yourself). Leave the name, address, and number where you can be reached beside the phone, along with numbers of two or three neighbors. Point out the emergency numbers posted on or near the phone. Give your sitter the checklist at right.

BABYSITTER'S CHECKLIST

Whether you're an experienced nanny or a high school student, babysitting is a big responsibility. The following safety checklist can help you.

■ Make sure you understand all instructions from parents. Ask questions as you need to.

■ Before parents leave, be sure that you can correctly spell and pronounce their full names and address. Write these down, as well as the family phone number (if not given on the telephone).

■ Do you have a phone number, as well as name and address, of where the parents will be? Make sure that you also have several neighbors' phone numbers and that emergency numbers are taped to the telephone or kept beside it.

■ Ask for a tour of the house. Watch for and ask about any hazards. Discuss any special fire escape routes.

■ While alone with small children, watch them. Don't leave a baby, even for a minute, where he or she could fall (such as on a changing table or sofa).

■ Unless the parent asks you to, do not give babies and small children a bath. (If you do, stay with them every minute.) Don't let the kids swim in a swimming pool, either.

■ If the phone rings, ask to take a message without saying that the parents are out. Keep exterior doors locked. If the doorbell rings, do not open the door to a stranger.

■ In the event of fire, take the children out of the house immediately and then call the fire department from a neighbor's house or call box.

■ If you suspect accidental poisoning of one of the kids, call the poison control center, hospital emergency room, or pediatrician immediately.

■ Call the emergency room or pediatrician in case of a medical emergency, such as choking or a bad cut. Call the parents as soon as possible.

Make sure you know where to reach parents in case of an emergency.

Index

Resources for Further Information

- **AAA Traffic Safety Department**
  8111 Gatehouse Road
  Falls Church, VA 22047

- **American Academy of Pediatrics**
  141 N. W. Point Road
  P.O. Box 927
  Elk Grove Village, IL 60007

- **American Red Cross National Headquarters**
  17th & D Streets, N.W.
  Washington, D.C. 20006

- **National Highway Traffic Safety Administration**
  400 7th Street, S.W.
  Washington, D.C. 20590

- **National Safety Council**
  444 N. Michigan Avenue, Dept. P.R.
  Chicago, IL 60611

- **U.S. Consumer Product Safety Commission**
  Washington, D.C. 20207
  (800) 638-2772